Short Prayers for the Long Day

Also by Giles Harcourt:
Dawn through our Darkness

SHORT PRAYERS FOR THE LONG DAY

Compiled by

GILES AND MELVILLE HARCOURT

COLLINS

Collins Liturgical Publications
8 Grafton Street, London W1X 3LA

Distributed in USA by
Harper & Row, Publishers, Inc., San Francisco
Icehouse One — 401
151 Union Street, San Francisco, CA 94111-1299

Distributed in Canada by
Novalis, Box 9700, Terminal,
375 Rideau St, Ottawa, Ontario K1G 4B4

Distributed in Ireland by
Educational Company of Ireland
21 Talbot Street, Dublin 1

Collins Liturgical Australia
PO Box 316, Blackburn, Victoria 3130

Collins Liturgical New Zealand
PO Box 1, Auckland

ISBN 0 00 599592 02

First Published 1978
Eighth Printing 1987
© Compilation 1978 Giles and Melville Harcourt

Made and printed in Great Britain
by William Collins Sons and Co, Glasgow

CONTENTS

Contents

2. NOON

3. NIGHT

Contents

ACKNOWLEDGEMENTS

This book has been compiled over a lifetime of ministry and prayer. Every effort has been made to trace the copyright owners of material included in it. However, the authors and publishers would be grateful if any omissions in these acknowledgements could be brought to their attention, for correction in future editions.

The permission of the following is gratefully acknowledged:

Anglican Church of Canada, for texts from *Experiment and Liturgy*. Cambridge and Oxford University Presses, for the texts from *New English Bible*, second edition © 1970. James Clarke & Co. Ltd., for H. E. Fosdick, *Assurance of Immortality*. Collins Publishers, Fontana Books for prayers by Rita Snowden. Church Missionary Society, for 'Lord show us how deeply', prayer used at CWME Assembly, Bangkok 1973, and for 'So the Master of the garden', from Eric Hague, *In the Shadow of the Nine Dragons*. Curtis Brown, Australia, and Roger Bush, for *Prayers for Pagans*. Darton Longman & Todd, for extracts from *Catholic Prayer Book*. Darton Longman & Todd and Doubleday & Co. Inc., for text from *Jerusalem Bible*. Darton Longman & Todd and Griffin Press, for Jean Vanier, *Tears of Silence*. Faber & Faber Ltd., for texts from T. S. Eliot, *Murder in the Cathedral* and *Collected Poems 1909–1962*; Dag Hammarskjold, *Markings*, translated by Lief Sjoberg and W. H. Auden; W. H. Auden, *Collected Longer Poems*. Monica Furlong. Alan Gaunt, *New Prayers for Worship*, John Paul, The Preachers Press, Charlton House, Hounslet Rd, Leeds. Gill and Macmillan Ltd, for texts by Michel Quoist. Victor Gollancz Ltd, for Dorothy Sayers, *The Man Born to be King*. William Heinemann Ltd, for Malcolm Boyd, *Are You Running With Me Jesus?* Hodder & Stoughton Ltd, for Frank Colquhoun, *Parish Prayers*, and 'Peace does not mean' by G. A. Studdert-Kennedy. The Trustees of the Tagore Estate and Macmillan London and Basingstoke for 'This is my prayer to thee' from *Collected Poems and Plays of Rabindranath Tagore*. A. R. Mowbray & Co. Ltd., for N. Goodacre, *Prayers for Today*. New American Library, for extracts from *The Way of Life* by Lau Tzu, translated by R. B. Blakney. Copyright © 1955 Raymond B. Blakney. Oxford University Press, for G. K. Chesterton, 'O God of earth and altar'; S. C. Lowry, 'Son of God, Eternal Saviour' (verse 2). David Scott, for 'Blessed be the roof of stars'. Sidgwick and Jackson, for John Masefield, *The Everlasting Mercy*. SPCK for Edward Sedding, 'Jesus Lord and Brother', from *The Hidden Garden of Prayer*; and for 'Eternal God and Father', from *The Daily Office* of The Joint Liturgical Group. SCM Press Ltd, for Walter Rauschenbusch, *A Book of Prayers for Schools*. M. B. Yeats, Miss Anne Yeats and the Macmillan Co. of London and Basingstoke, for 'A Prayer for Old Age', from *The Collected Poems of W. B. Yeats*.

FOREWORD

There is a great deal of evidence that men and women in our society are anxious to learn about prayer. Any help that can be given is, so I have discovered, very welcome. This book will be a great help to many people.

Many of us need to use a text when we pray, but it is important to use texts sensibly. Sometimes they do not express exactly what we want to say ourselves but they provide a starting point.

Our part is to approach our prayer in a relaxed manner and then be sensitive to the fact that God Himself will intervene in order to enable us to dwell perhaps for a few moments in His presence. Those moments are to be relished and enjoyed.

September 1977   George Basil, Cardinal Hume

PREFACE

This small book – divided symbolically into Morning, Noon and Night – is a compilation of prayers (including reflections and meditations) that have been loved and used by many people of all ages and at various times, and may conceivably be helpful to others who feel the need of prayer in a day when God is scarcely the most popular Being in the Universe. It makes no claim to be comprehensive. Could such a book ever be? But the compilers hope it may, now and then, be helpful to someone at some time. Prayer is the first language of the heart and, as such, it transcends time, place, caste or race to touch the very core of existence.

Prayer, of course, may be silent, its wording known only to the individual; but if, on the other hand, it is spoken or read then its structure, as we well know, can range from elaborate liturgies and litanies to the naive utterances of a small child. Indeed we are inclined to think God may favour the latter, for are we not bidden 'to become as little children' that we may inherit the Kingdom of Heaven.

Do not let us, in our attempts to be 'with it', dismiss the simpler ways and expressions of other ages. It might help to remember that it is the heart of man that interests God, not his poetry; although admittedly great poetry has often inspired great living, and it has certainly been an aid to much personal devotion. But whether we pray to God through the language of a Saint Augustine, a George Herbert, a Michel Quoist or through the less-skilled sentences of more ordinary men and women, or even in our own halting words, *the important thing is to pray*, to pray with our heart; and possibly the structured prayer, created by genius or profound fervour, may help to give the heart more depth and thereby more genuine freedom.

GILES AND MELVILLE HARCOURT

Some men can see life clean and flickering all around,
And some can see only what they are shown;
Some men look straight into the eyes of the gods,
And some men can see no gods,
They only know the gods are there because of the gleam
On the face of the men who see.

D. H. Lawrence

MORNING

Every morning a new world is born;
Every day a new chance.

I

GOD

In the universe, law;
In the conscience, goodness;
In the mind, truth;
In nature and art, beauty and order;
In the heart, love.

      Bradford Smith, *What is God?*

I am the image of God: therefore if
  God would see Himself, He must look down, and see
Himself in me.

      Angelus Silesius 1624–77

I believe in the sun even when it is not shining.
I believe in love even when I cannot feel it.
I believe in God, even when he is silent.

      Written on a wall by a
      Jewish prisoner in Cologne

Let me be quiet now, and kneel,
  Who never knelt before,
Here, where the leaves paint patterns light
  On a leaf-strewn forest floor;
For I, who saw no God at all
  In sea or earth or air,
Baptised by Beauty, now look up
  To see God everywhere.

      Ellen Francis Gilbert

A lonely walk,
A quiet talk,
A grain of sand,
A soft white hand,
A child's new toy,
A moment's joy,
A new day's dawn,
A tottering fawn,
A cloud above,
Spring's young love,
A breath of air,
A silent prayer,
A gentle nod,
This is God.

Robert M. Warner, *This is God*

Thank you for the tranquil night.
Thank you for the stars.
Thank you for the silence.

Thank you for the time you have given me.
Thank you for life.
Thank you for grace.

Thank you for being there, Lord.
Thank you for listening to me, for taking me seriously,
    for gathering my gifts in your hands
    to offer them to your Father.
Thank you, Lord,
Thank you.

Michel Quoist 1918–

Lord thou knowest how busy I must be today.
If I forget thee do not thou forget me.   AMEN

Lord Astley at the Battle of Edgehill, 1642

Morning: God

If Chance can dance the dust afar
in myriad motions to a star,
If Chance can mould with pollen gold
the silken seeds where lilies are,
If Chance one daisy can unfold
then God the hand of Chance must hold.

All things exist
Only in thy light, and thy glory is declared even in that which
    denies thee; the darkness declares the glory of light.
Those who deny thee could not deny, if thou didst not exist;
    and their denial is never complete, for if it were so,
    they would not exist.

T. S. Eliot 1888–1965, *Murder in the Cathedral*

It is not the image we create of God which proves God;
it's the effort we make to create this image.

Arise early, serve God devoutly, and the world busily.
Do thy work wisely, give thine alms secretly; go to thy ways gravely.
Answer the people demurely, go to thy meat appetitely,
Sit thereat discreetly, arise temperately.
Go to thy supper soberly, and to thy bed merrily.
Be in thine inn jocundly.
Please thy love duly, and sleep surely.

Sulpicius c. 363–420

UNIVERSE

O God, we thank thee for this universe, our great home; for its vastness and its riches, and for the manifold life which teems upon it and of which we are part. We praise thee for the arching sky and the blessed winds, for the driving clouds and the constellations on high. We praise thee for the salt sea and the running water, for the everlasting hills, for the trees, and for the grass under our feet. We thank thee for our senses by which we can see the splendour of the morning, and hear the songs of birds, and enjoy the smells of the springtime. Grant us, we pray thee, a heart wide open to all this joy and beauty, and save our souls from being so steeped in care or so darkened by passion that we pass heedless and unseeing when even the thorn-bush by the wayside is aflame with the glory of God.   AMEN

Walter Rauschenbusch

The day returns and brings us the petty round of irritating concerns and duties. Help us to play the man, help us to perform them with laughter and kind faces; let cheerfulness abound with industry. Give us to go blithely on our business all this day; bring us to our resting bed weary and content and undishonoured, and grant us in the end the gift of sleep.   AMEN

R. L. Stevenson 1850–94

Why should I myself hasten to answer every riddle which life offers me? I am well assured that the Great Questioner, who brings me so many problems, will bring the answer also in due time.

R. W. Emerson 1803–82

To abandon religion for science is merely to fly from one region of faith to another.

Morning: Universe

O thou, who art the true sun of the world, ever-rising, and never going down; who by thy most wholesome appearing and sight dost nourish and gladden all things in heaven and earth; we beseech thee mercifully to shine into our hearts, that the night and darkness of sin, and the mists of error on every side, being driven away by the brightness of thy shining within our hearts, we may all our life walk without stumbling, as in the daytime, and being pure and clean from the works of darkness, may abound in all good works which thou hadst prepared for us to walk in.   AMEN

Erasmus 1466–1546

Dear Father,
for whom the beauty of your world
became the medium of the incarnation,
grant us the power, through newly-awakened senses,
to respond to the beautiful in our daily lives –
whether within the familiar frame of household chores
or the majesty of Nature's changing moods.
May we see it in the dancing eyes of a happy child,
in the sweat-gleaming muscles of toiling workmen;
let it touch our heart and ear
through the careless laughter of young girlhood,
and the quiet wisdom of silvered age.
Teach us to recognize it in Autumn's scudding clouds,
in the liquid grace of gliding fish
and the restrained strength of a champing horse.
But more especially, sweet God, may the manifestations of your beauty
be most truly seen in high thought,
in the sacrificial life, the spontaneous gesture,
the encouraging smile, the patient ear, the apt word –
all of which are but a reflection
of the peerless life of your blessed Son, Jesus Christ,
whose sorrow was turned to joy
and for whom death was defeated in the resurrection.

Melville Harcourt 1909–

God, we thank you that you have made the countryside so beautiful. As we think of hills and valleys, or rivers and waterfalls, woods, open moorlands, little lanes and wide stretching meadows, we ask you to give us and all who use them such a true sense of values that we may help to keep them beautiful and unspoilt.   AMEN

To thy tender loving care, O Heavenly Father, we commend all who travel on the highways of the sea. Ever give to them the assurance of thine ancient promise that when they pass through the waters thou wilt be with them, and if it be thy gracious will, bring them to the haven where they would be; for the sake of Jesus Christ, thy Son, our Lord.   AMEN

3

NATURE

O God, of whose love comes sunshine and flowers, great spreading trees, sunset and dawn, and all the wondrous pageantry of the changing year, we praise thee that thou dost come to us through all the beauty of thy world. We thank thee for sudden swift glimpses of thy beauty: a sudden sight of flowers in city streets, raindrops shining in the sun: cobwebs gemmed with dew; stars reflected in a roadside puddle; shadows moving up a glassy slope; leafy trees in the lamplight; green moss on a stone wall; the sun on the bark of a fir tree. For these and all sudden showings of thy beauty we praise and adore thee.

Creator of life and light, we bless thee for the beauty of the world; we thank thee for physical joy; for the ecstasy of swift motion; for deep water to swim in; for the goodly smell of rain on dry ground; for hills to climb and hard work to do; for music that lifts our hearts in one breath to heaven; for all thy sacraments of beauty and joy, we thank thee, Lord.

O most high, almighty, good Lord God, to thee be long praise, glory, honour and all blessing!

Praised be my Lord God with all his creatures, and especially our brother the sun, who brings us the day and brings us the light; fair is he and shines with a great splendour; O Lord, he signifies to us thee.

Praised be my Lord for our sister the moon, and for the stars, the which he has set clear and lovely in the heaven.

Praised be my Lord for our brother the wind, and for air and cloud, calms and all weather, by the which thou upholdest life in all creatures.

Praised be my Lord for our sister water, who is very serviceable unto us and humble and precious and clean.

Praised be my Lord for our brother fire, through whom thou givest light in the darkness; and he is bright and pleasant and very mighty and strong.

Praised be my Lord for our mother the earth, the which doth sustain us and keep us, and bringest forth divers fruit and flowers of many colours and grass.

Praise ye and bless ye the Lord, and give thanks unto him, and serve him with great humility.　　AMEN

St Francis of Assisi 1181-1226

Beloved God of the woods and streams, grant us to be beautiful in the inner man, and all we have of outer things to be at peace with those within. Counting only the wise to be truly rich, increase to all who here abide their store of gold.

Plato BC 427-BC 347

4
ANIMALS

Hear our humble prayer, O God, for our friends the animals,
especially for animals who are suffering; for all that are overworked
and underfed and cruelly treated; for all wistful creatures in captivity
that beat against their bars; for any that are hunted or lost or deserted
or frightened or hungry; for all that are in pain or dying; for all that
must be put to death. We entreat for them all thy mercy and pity, and
for those who deal with them we ask a heart of compassion and gentle
hands and kindly words. Make us ourselves to be true friends to
animals and so to share the blessing of the merciful. For the sake of
thy Son the tenderhearted, Jesus Christ, our Lord.   AMEN

12/89   **Russian Prayer**

> Little things that run and quail
> And die in silence and despair!
>
> Little things, that fight, and fail,
> And fall on earth and sea and air!
>
> All trapped and frightened little things,
> The mouse, the coney, hear our prayer!
>
> As we forgive those done to us,
> – the lamb, the linnet and the hare –
>
> Forgive us all our trespasses,
> Little creatures everywhere!

Lord Jesus Christ, who has taught us that without our Father in
heaven no sparrow falls to the ground, help us to be very kind to all
animals, and to our pets. May we remember that you will one day
ask us if we have been good to them. Bless us as we take care of them;
for your mercy's sake.

He prayeth well who loveth well
Both man and bird and beast;
He prayeth best who loveth best
All things both great and small,
For the dear God who loveth us
He made and loveth all.   12/88

William Blake 1757–1827

There be four things which are little upon the earth, but they are
exceeding wise: the ants are a people not strong, yet they prepare
their meat in the summer; the conies are but a feeble folk, yet make
they their houses in the rocks; the locusts have no king, yet go they
forth all of them by bands; the spider taketh hold with her hands, and
is in kings' palaces.

Proverbs 30:24–8 (AV)

O Lord of all creatures, make the man, my master, as faithful to other
men as I am to him. Make him as loving to his family and friends as
I am to him. Make him the honest guardian of the blessings which
you have entrusted to him as I honestly guard his own.

Give him, O Lord, an easy and spontaneous smile, easy and
spontaneous as when I wag my tail. May he be as readily grateful
as I am quick to lick his hand. Grant him patience equal to mine, when
I await his return without complaining. Give him my courage, my
readiness to sacrifice everything for him in all circumstances, even life
itself. Keep for him the youthfulness of my heart and the cheerfulness
of my thoughts. O Lord of all creatures, as I am always truly a dog,
grant that he may be always truly a man.   AMEN

O Lord our God, who hatest nothing that thou hast made, keep us
from all cruelty to beasts, birds or any of thy creatures. May we
always remember that thou hast made both them and us, and show
them the mercy that we have received from thee; for thy Name's
sake.   AMEN

A robin redbreast in a cage
puts all heaven in a rage.
A skylark wounded in the wing
doth make a cherub cease to sing.
He who shall hurt the little wren
shall never be beloved by men.

William Blake 1757–1827

O thou Little Brother, that brimmest with full heart, and having
naught, possessest all, surely thou dost well to sing! For thou hast life
without labour, and beauty without burden, and riches without care.
When thou wakest, lo, it is dawn; and when thou comest to sleep it
is eve. And when thy two wings lie folded about thy heart, lo, there
is rest. Therefore sing, Brother, having this great wealth, that when
thou singest thou givest thy riches to all.

St Francis of Assisi 1181–1226

5

QUEST

The bliss of growth,
the glory of action,
the splendour of beauty,
for yesterday is but a dream,
and tomorrow is only a vision.
But TODAY well-lived makes
every yesterday a dream of happiness
and every tomorrow a vision of hope.
Look well therefore to this day!
Such is the salutation of the dawn.

From the Sanskrit

Morning: Quest

First, birth:
the beginning:
the start of the way.

Then infancy:
an easy time,
without a burden on your back.

Then childhood:
a happy road of flowers,
when all is gay and careless.

Then youth:
when you hope, and dream, and love.

Then maturity:
when cares set in,
and you may lose your joy of God
for love of earthly things.

Then age:
the end of earthly bondage,
and the sound of trumpets you discern
for the wanderer's return.

Michael Welsh, aged 12

God, set our hearts at liberty from the service of ourselves, and let it
be our meat and drink to do your will:
through Jesus Christ our Lord.   AMEN

The beauty of life is to be found
not in luxury, but in simplicity;
In sweat of the brow, sweat of the hands, sweat of the heart;
in pride of work, without greed of gold.
To be loyal in friendship, patient in suffering, and rich in laughter
is to be a good comrade in the workshop of life,
and to such faithful servants God will pay wages of peace and joy.

Short Prayers for the Long Day

Thou who art over us,
Thou who art one of us,
Thou who art –
Also within us,
May all see thee – in me also,
May I prepare the way for thee,
May I thank thee for all that shall fall to my lot.
May I also not forget the needs of others,
Keep me in thy love
As thou wouldest that all should be kept in mine.
May everything in this my being be directed to thy glory
and may I never despair.
For I am under thy hand,
And in thee is all power and goodness.

Give me a pure heart – that I may see thee,
A humble heart – that I may hear thee,
A heart of love – that I may serve thee,
A heart of faith – that I may abide in thee.

Dag Hammarskjold 1905–61, *Markings*

Incomparable God
you have made yourself
available to us
in all your power
and all your love.

You have put the world at our feet
and made us lords of your creation.

Now we go out to the adventure of living
in good heart
and with high hope
because you are going with us.

Alan Gaunt

Lord, we pray thee that thou wilt open our eyes to behold the heaven that lies about us, wherein they walk who, being born to the new life, serve thee with the clearer vision and the greater joy; through Jesus Christ our Saviour.   AMEN

6/89

> But once I pass this way,
> and then – no more.
> But once – and then, the Silent Door
> swings on its hinges,
> Opens . . . Closes –
> and no more
> I pass this way.
> So while I may,
> with all my might
> I will assay
> sweet comfort and delight
> to all I meet upon the Pilgrim Way.
> For no one travels twice the Great Highway
> that climbs through darkness up to light
> through night
> to day.

I shall pass through this world but once.
Therefore any good that I can do, any kind act
that I can perform for any fellow-creature, let me do it now.
Let me not delay, or omit it, for I shall not pass this way again.

> attributed to
> Etienne Giennet 18th cent.

> Lord, what we have not, give us.
> Lord, what we know not, teach us.
> Lord, what we are not, make us.
> Forgive what we have been.
> Sanctify what we are.
> And order what we shall be.
> For your mercy's sake.   AMEN

Short Prayers for the Long Day

What do I owe to those who follow me?
To build more sure the freedom we have won:
To build more sure the kingdoms of thy grace,
Kingdoms secure in truth and righteousness.

John Oxenham 1852–1941

Where are you going, Lord?
I'm going to Bethlehem to be born a child:
Lord, let me come too . . .

Where are you going, Lord?
I'm going to Galilee to grow as a boy!
Lord, let me come too . . .

Where are you going, Lord?
I'm walking through Israel, to learn life while I'm young:
Lord, let me come too . . .

Where are you going, Lord?
I'm going to Jerusalem to face life, like a man:
Lord, let me come too . . .

Where are you going, Lord?
I'm reaching out into the world, on my Cross, for you:
Lord, let me come too . . .

Giles Harcourt 1936–

Let us serve God and be cheerful for his honour and glory.   AMEN

Bishop Hacket 17th century

Lord, enlarge the sphere of our human experience to make the loving
of those around us a daily part of our living, to spread happiness if
we can, allay violence if we must, and administer gentle understanding wherever problems are to be found, through Jesus Christ
our friend and Saviour.   AMEN

Giles Harcourt 1936–

May the strength of God pilot us;
may the power of God preserve us;
may the wisdom of God instruct us;
may the hand of God protect us;
may the way of God direct us;
may the shield of God defend us;
may the host of God guard us against the snares of evil and the
    temptation of the world;
may Christ be with us, Christ before us, Christ in us, Christ over us;
may Thy salvation, O Lord, be always ours, this day and for evermore.

attributed to St Patrick 389–461

Lord, Lord, do you hear me?
Lord, show me my door,
take me by the hand.
Open the door,
show me the way,
the path leading to joy, to light.

Michel Quoist 1918–

O Lord, grant that each one who has to do with us today may be the happier for it. Let it be given us each hour today what we shall say, and grant us the wisdom of a loving heart that we may say the right thing rightly. Help us to enter into the mind of every one who talks with us and keep us alive to the feelings of others. Give us a quick eye for little kindnesses, that we may be ready in doing them, and gracious in receiving them. Give us quick perception of the feelings and needs of others, and make us eager-hearted in helping them. For Christ's sake. AMEN

L. H. M. Soulby

Take no thought of the harvest
But only of proper sowing.

T. S. Eliot 1888–1965

Cause me to hear thy loving kindness in the morning;
For in thee do I trust:
Cause me to know the way wherein I should walk;
For I lift up my soul to thee.
Teach me to do thy will;
For thou art my God
Let thy loving Spirit lead me.

Psalm 143

Lord, make the old tolerant,
the young sympathetic,
the great humble,
the busy patient,
Make rich people understanding,
strong people gentle,
those who are weak prayerful;
make the religious lovable,
happy folk thoughtful,
the clever kindly,
the bad good,
the good pleasant
and, dear Lord, make me what I ought to be.

I ask for daily bread, but not for wealth, lest I forget the poor.
I ask for strength, but not for power, lest I despise the meek.
I ask for wisdom, but not for learning, lest I condemn the simple.
I ask for a clean name, but not for fame, lest I condemn the lowly.
I ask for peace of mind, but not for idle hours, lest I fail to hearken
   to the call of duty.

Inazo Nitobe

As a man is so's his God; this word
Explains why God's so oft absurd.

I laid me down and slept;
I awaked; for the Lord sustained me.

30

If I can do some good today,
if I can serve along life's way,
if I can something helpful say,
Lord, show me how.

If I can right a human wrong,
if I can help to make one strong,
if I can cheer with smile or song,
Lord, show me how.

If I can aid one in distress,
if I can make a burden less,
if I can spread more happiness.
Lord, show me how.

Grenville Kleiser

6

CHILDHOOD

I have seen the greatest saints, says God. But I tell you
I have never seen anything so funny,
and I therefore know
of nothing so beautiful in the world,
as that child going to sleep while he says his prayers
(as that little creature going to sleep in all confidence)
and getting his Our Father mixed up with his Hail Mary.
Nothing is so beautiful and it is even one point
on which the Blessed Virgin agrees with me.
And I can even say it is the only point on which we agree.
Because as a rule we disagree,
she being for mercy,
whereas I, of course, have to be for justice.

Charles Péguy 1873–1914

31

Short Prayers for the Long Day

If a child lives with criticism
he learns to condemn.
If a child lives with ridicule
he learns to be shy.
If a child lives with tolerance
he learns to be patient.
If a child lives with encouragement
he learns to have confidence.
If a child lives with fairness
he learns justice.
If a child lives with approval
he learns to know himself.
If a child lives with love around him
he learns to bring love into the world.

Church Book Room Press

To reserve time and fresh energy for my children,
so that I can be their close and interested friend –
To fit my children to meet life and people
bravely, honestly and independently –
To give my children freedom, but
to teach them how to use that freedom,
so that they will not confuse liberty with license –
To show my warm love for my children
as well as conscientiously care for them –
To manage them with intelligence and affection,
and not by punishment, condemnation,
fear, fault-finding and nagging –
To guide my children instead of driving them –
To direct their energy instead of repressing it –
To try to understand my children
instead of sitting in judgement on them –
And through all misdemeanours both trivial and serious
to love them steadfastly.

Gladys Huntington Bevans

Thank you, Lord, for making me so small.
I enjoyed the large room
and all the large people.

But why, Lord, when I spoke to them
did they smile and speak to each other?
Why were their words, their cups, their saucers,
their sips, their laughs and their voices, bigger than mine?

I spoke of football; so they spoke of Bach.
I talked of schooldays; so they mentioned wine.
I longed to be loved; so they patted the sofa, and then the dog.

All I suggested, they countered:
all I tried, they loved to ignore.
Lord, I have lived only in days, but they in years
I know so little, they so much.
But, unlike them,
I can eat more little cakes without getting fat.
I can climb more little stairs without getting puffed.
I can sleep more soundly than they who need pills.

Perhaps Lord, one day I shall be like them, but I pray not.
Meanwhile I am most thankful, Good Lord,
for you making me so small, else how could I see
what is really in this large room,
with all these large people
who are really – quite small.   Giles Harcourt 1936–

        God who created me
        nimble and light of limb,
        in three elements free,
        to run, to ride, to swim;
        Not when the sense is dim,
        but now, from the heart of joy,
        I would remember him;
        Take the thanks of a boy.
                        H. C. Beeching

Holy God, who madest me
and all things else to worship thee;
Keep me fit in mind and heart,
Body and soul to take my part.
Fit to stand, fit to run,
fit for sorrow, fit for fun;
Fit to work and fit to play,
fit to face life day by day;
Holy God, who madest me,
make me fit to worship thee.

7

YOUTH

God, who has enabled Youth to see visions, and Age to dream
dreams, help both young and old to understand each other. May
those who are young be always courteous to the aged, and never
resent the teaching of experience or the restraint of discipline. May
those who are older look with sympathy upon new ideas, and control
the young with love that encourages and not with fear that represses,
so that all, both young and old, may work together for the founding
of your kingdom, for the sake of Jesus Christ our Lord.   AMEN

Happy, crying, dirty, clean or sad,
they are our tomorrow and yours.
And that kid with the club foot, what will he be?
Teacher, doctor (for I can still see him)
Or outcast because he is different.
For you were once a different child, an outcast.
Grant us to see our responsibility to you, in them,
Your tomorrow and ours.   AMEN

Roger Bush, *Prayers for Pagans*

Blessed be God who hath sent his Son to live our human life: who as a Father knows our human frame, pitying our weakness, giving help in time of need; in sorrow, comfort; in temptation, strength; and in death the sure and certain hope of life eternal. Blessed be God.

Lord of all power and might, we praise you for your good gifts of health and strength, for the sight of our eyes, the hearing of our ears, the strength of our limbs, the power of our minds, and the energy which forges them into a fit instrument for your service. Praise to you, God of our health.   AMEN

Youth is not a time of life. It is a state of mind. It is not a matter of ripe cheeks, red lips and supple knees. It is a temper of the will, a quality of the imagination, a vigour of the emotions. It is a freshness of the deep things in life.

Youth means a temperamental predominance of courage over timidity, of the appetite for adventure over love of ease. And this often exists in a man of fifty more than a youth of twenty.

Nobody grows old merely by living a number of years. People grow old only by deserting their ideals. Years wrinkle their skin, but to give up enthusiasm wrinkles the soul. Worry, doubt, self-distrust, fear and despair – these are the long, long years that bow the head and turn the growing spirit back to dust.

Whether seventy or seventeen, there is in every being's heart the love of wonder, the sweet amazement of the stars and star-like things and thoughts, the undaunted challenge of events, the unfailing child-like appetite for what next, and the joy and game of life.

You are as young as your faith, as old as your doubt; as young as your self-confidence, as old as your fears; as young as your hope, as old as your despair.

In the central place of your heart there is a radio station. So long as it receives messages of beauty, hope, cheer, courage, grandeur and power from the earth, from man, and from the infinite, so long are you young. But when the wires are all down, and the central place of your heart is covered with the snows of pessimism and the ice of cynicism, then you are grown old – very old indeed. And may God have mercy on your soul.

8
EDUCATION

We teach religion all day long.
We teach it in arithmetic, by accuracy.
We teach it in language, by learning to say what we mean – yea, yea or nay, nay.
We teach it in history, by humanity.
We teach it in geography, by breadth of mind.
We teach it in handicraft, by thoroughness.
We teach it in astronomy, by reverence.
We teach it by good manners to one another, and by truthfulness in all things.
We teach students to build the Church of Christ out of the actual relationships in which they stand to their teachers and to their schoolfellows.

Deliver us, O God, from following the fashions of the day in our thinking. Save us from the worship of science, and grant that, giving thee thanks for the skill of the scientist, we may be preserved from the abuse of his discoveries. Help us never to confuse any creature with the Creator, or man with God. May we acknowledge man's reason as thy gift, and, being freed from all false hopes and misplaced trust, find in thee our hope and our salvation; through Jesus Christ our Lord.

Parish Prayers, edited by Frank Colquhoun

Glory be to thee, O Lord, for that thou didst create not only the visible light, but the light invisible, that which may be known of God, the law written in the heart;

Give us a mind to perceive this light in the oracles of prophets, the melody of psalms, the prudence of proverbs, the experience of histories, and the life and love of our Lord Jesus Christ, for his sake.

Bishop Lancelot Andrewes 1555–1626

God of Truth, who hast guided men in knowledge throughout the ages, and from whom every good thought cometh, help us in our study to use thy gifts of wisdom and knowledge. Let us read good books carefully, and listen to all wise teaching humbly that we may be led into all truth, and strengthened in all the goodness of life, to the praise of thy holy name.   AMEN

Rowland Williams 19th century (adapted)

We beseech thee, O God, the God of Truth
That what we know not of things we ought to know thou wilt
   teach us.
That what we know of Truth thou wilt keep us therein.
That what we are mistaken in, as men must be, thou wilt correct.
That at whatsoever truths we stumble thou wilt yet establish us.
And from all things that are false and from all knowledge that would
   be hurtful, thou wilt evermore deliver us,
Through Jesus Christ our Lord.   AMEN

St Fulgentius 468–533

For when the ONE GREAT SCORER comes
To write against your name,
He marks – not that you won or lost,
But how you played the game.

Grantland Rice 1880–

9

FELLOWSHIP

All our loved ones we commend
Lord, to Thee, man's truest friend;
Guard and guide them to the end,
we beseech Thee, Jesus.

Short Prayers for the Long Day

Ugly people,
dirty people,
ignorant people,
stupid people,
weak people.

Arrogant people,
selfish people,
pompous people,
smug people,
too-clever-by-half people.

There are so many people
we can despise
or envy
or even hate
and feel quite justified.

Lord,
we have put up our defences
and you are going to need
all your ingenuity
all your patience
and all your skill
to break through our castle walls;
and when you have
we'll make a last ditch stand
and fight to the death
to prove to you
that we have been right all along.

But meanwhile, Lord,
please win a few of the skirmishes.
Prevail on us to reach out,
however timidly,
to touch the untouchable.

Morning: Fellowship

Entice us
by some means
to come out from behind our barricades
and expose ourselves to danger,
as you came, in Christ
from behind the barricades of heaven
to be among us,
vulnerable,
the object of prejudice
and cruelty.

Let love break in
and steal our prize possession,
pride,
and crush our fear
with confidence.

Let it be so, Lord,
for Jesus' sake.

Alan Gaunt

O God, from whose love neither time nor space can separate us, we thank you that those who are absent from us are still present with you. We trust them to your loving care, knowing that underneath are the everlasting arms, only beseeching you to grant that both they and we, by drawing nearer you, may be drawn nearer to one another, through Jesus Christ our Lord. AMEN

I am glad you made my neighbour different from me;
    a different coloured skin,
    a different shaped face,
    a different response to you.
I need my neighbour to teach me about you.
He knows all the things I don't know.

Monica Furlong

O God, bless our home, our family, friends, and neighbours,
and give us thankful hearts for all thy mercies.   AMEN

Prayers, New and Old

Father of men, in whom are one
all humankind beneath the sun,
stablish our work in thee begun.
Except the house be built of thee,
in vain the builder's toil must be;
O strengthen our infirmity!
Man lives not for himself alone,
in others' good he finds his own,
life's worth in fellowship is known.
We, friends and comrades on life's way,
gather within these walls to pray;
bless thou our fellowship today.

H. C. Shuttleworth

Holy Father, in thy mercy,
Hear our anxious prayer;
Keep our loved ones, now far absent,
'Neath thy care.

When in sorrow, when in danger,
When in loneliness,
In thy love look down and comfort
their distress.

Holy Spirit, let thy teaching
sanctify their life;
Send thy grace, that they may conquer
in the strife.

I. Stephenson

O maker of us men, you have set us in no strange land, but surrounded our life with familiar things and well-known faces; we pray for all those amongst whom we live, our neighbours and acquaintances and those amongst whom we work, as well as our best friends and near relations. We cheerfully commit them all to your favour and care; pardon their sins, preserve them from all dangers of body and soul; and grant that we and they may ever dwell with you; through Jesus Christ our Lord. AMEN

J. Leslie Johnston

O Lord, teach us your children,
old and young,
large and small,
so to apply our Christian beliefs
to our daily living that
honesty and a generous spirit,
helpfulness and the wish to learn
become increasingly a part of us –
and so we a part of you. We ask it for
your Name's sake. AMEN

Giles Harcourt 1936–

The TV is my shepherd. My spiritual growth shall want!
It maketh me to sit down and do nothing for His name's sake –
    because it requireth all my attention . . .
It keepeth me from doing my duty as a Christian,
    because it presenteth to me so many things I must see . . .
It restoreth my knowledge of all things of the world
    and easily keepeth me away from the study of God's word . . .
It leadeth me from the paths of attending my Church
    and doing anything for the Kingdom of God.
Its sound and its pictures, they comfort me . . .
It offers me not the time to do the work of God . . .
American violence and commercials shall follow me all the days of my
    life;
And I'll take life second-hand from my Box in my own house for ever!

We praise Thee for the signs of Thy coming
   in the familiar world about us:
for the warmth and friendliness of home,
for the love that surrounds our comings and goings:
for the simple goodness of ordinary folk,
our friends, and the people we live with:
their generous thoughts and kindliness,
their quiet courage and sense of fun.

10

WORK

O Jesus, Master Carpenter of Nazareth, who on the cross, through
wood and nails worked man's whole salvation; wield well your tools
in this your workshop; that we who come to you rough-hewn may
by your hands be fashioned to a truer beauty and a greater usefulness:
for the honour of your holy name.   AMEN

Lord of all pots and pans and things; since I've no time to be
a saint by doing lovely things or watching late with Thee,
or dreaming in the dawnlight or storming heaven's gates,
make me a saint by getting meals, and washing up the plates.

Altho' I must have Martha's hands, I have a Mary mind:
And when I black the boots and shoes, Thy sandals, Lord, I find.
I think of how they trod the earth, each time I scrub the floor;
Accept this meditation, Lord, I haven't time for more.

Warm all the kitchen with Thy love, and light it with Thy peace;
Forgive me all my worrying, and make all grumbling cease.
Thou who didst love to give men food, in room or by the sea,
Accept this service that I do – I do it unto Thee.

Morning: Work

O God, I am Mustafah, the Tailor, and I work at the shop of Muhammed Ali. The whole day long I sit and pull the needle and the thread through the cloth. O God you are the needle and I am the thread. I am attached to you and I follow you. When the thread tries to slip away from the needle it becomes tangled up and must be cut so that it can be put back in the right place. O God, help me to follow you wherever you may lead me. For I am really only Mustafah, the Tailor, and I work at the shop of Muhammed Ali on the great square.

First prayer of a Muslim Convert

I want to begin this day with thankfulness, and continue it with eagerness.

I shall be busy; let me set about things in the spirit of service to you and to my fellows, that Jesus knew in the carpenter's shop in Nazareth.

I am glad that he drew no line between work sacred and secular.

Take the skill that resides in my hands, and use it today;

Take the experience that life has given me, and use it;

Keep my eyes open, and my imagination alert, that I may see how things look to others, especially the unwell, the worried, the over-worked. For your love's sake. AMEN

Rita Snowden

Jesus, Lord and brother,
at Nazareth you grew to manhood,
busy in the sunlit workshop with eye and hand and brain,
yet ever dreaming of a kingdom to be built,
worldwide, eternal, not made with hands:
Help us to grow in wisdom, loving the things of heaven,
seeing the world, as with your eyes, at its true value;
for the sake of yourself, our Saviour Jesus Christ. AMEN

Edward Sedding SS
(Mother Mary Clare SLG)

Short Prayers for the Long Day

Lord,
Give me
    busy hands,
    a sense of fun,
    an understanding heart,
    and peace in myself.

Help me
    to overcome my fears,
    to love you more,
    to accept love,
    and always to say the encouraging word.

Show me
    the beauty of a new day,
    the desolate spirit that cries for help,
    the satisfaction of simple living,
    how to make the loving gesture,
    and to see that every wrinkle hides some grace.

Lettie Harcourt 1909–

Teach me, my God and King,
In all things thee to see;
And what I do in anything,
    to do it as for thee.

All may of thee partake;
Nothing can be so mean,
which with this tincture 'for thy sake'
    will not grow bright and clean.

A servant with this clause,
makes drudgerie divine;
Who sweeps a room, as for thy laws,
    makes that and the action fine.

This is the famous stone,
that turneth all to gold;
For that which God doth teach and own
cannot for less be told.

George Herbert 1593–1633

II

CITY

O God, whose Son Jesus Christ wrought as a craftsman among the sons of men, we ask your blessing on all the toiling thousands of our cities. Grant to those who employ them a sense of justice and sympathy, and to those who labour a knowledge of the dignity and worth of their work. Keep us from prejudice of class or education, and help us to bring about a brotherhood of men, so that all may work gladly to build a city where slums are no more, oppression has ceased, competition is fair, and you may be ever glorified in praise and worship and work; through Jesus Christ our Lord. AMEN

My God, I heard this day,
That none doth build a stately habitation
But he that means to dwell therein.
What house more stately hath there been
Or can be than is man? To whose creation
All things are in decay.
Since then, my God, thou hast
So brave a palace built, O dwell in it,
That it may dwell with thee at last;
Till then afford us so much wit,
That, as the world serves us we may serve thee,
And both thy servants be.

George Herbert 1593–1633

Short Prayers for the Long Day

A thing of beauty is a joy forever;
Its loveliness increases; it will never
Pass into nothingness; but still will keep
A bower quiet for us, and a sleep
Full of sweet dreams, and health, and quiet breathing.
Therefore, on every morrow, are we wreathing
A flowery band to bind us to the earth.

John Keats 1795–1821

O God, grant us a vision of our city, fair as she might be; a city of justice, where none shall prey on others; a city of plenty, where vice and poverty shall cease to fester; a city of brotherhood, where all success shall be founded on service, and honour shall be given to nobleness alone; a city of peace, where order shall not rest on force, but on the love of all for the city, the great mother of the common life and weal. Hear thou, O Lord, the silent prayer of all our hearts as we each pledge our time and strength and thought to speed the day of her coming beauty and righteousness.   AMEN

Walter Rauschenbusch

Unless the Lord keepeth the city
the watchman waketh in vain.

Psalm 127:2

A nameless and indifferent crowd, probably far from you, Lord.
   I am one with the crowd, and I see why it's sometimes hard for me to rise higher.
   This crowd is heavy-laden soles on my feet, my slow feet – a crowd too large for my overburdened skiff.
   Yet, Lord, I have no right to overlook these people; they are my brothers,
   And I cannot save myself, alone.

Michel Quoist 1918–

46

It's only when I look at others, Lord, I begin to see how rich I am.
Seen the slums? The soup kitchen line-ups?
The city missions? The barefoot ragged kids in the park?
The wealth is yours, Lord.
The glittering gold that backs the dollars and cents we use each day.
How have we messed up the distribution?
What sort of steward have I been of the wealth you've given me?
Help me confess my carelessness.
What have I offered you, Lord,
Not in cash, perhaps, but
In honesty in my dealings?
In trusteeship?
Teach me, Lord, that I am using your bounty, your gifts,
And bless me as I become aware of my responsibility.   AMEN

Roger Bush, *Prayers for Pagans*

Lord, I pray:

That men may increasingly work together in agreement, doing things that are sane to do, with mutual helpfulness, temperance and toleration.

That the great masses of humanity may rise out of base and immediate anxieties, out of dwarfing pressures and cramped surroundings, to understanding and participation and fine effort;

That the resources of the earth may be husbanded and harvested, economised and used with scientific skill for the maximum of human benefit.

That towns and cities may be finely built and men and women finely bred and taught and trained;

That there may be open ways and peace and freedom from end to end of the earth;

That through the great body of mankind may go evermore an increasing common understanding, an intensifying brotherhood.

AMEN

Prayers for the City of God

God of the city, God of the tenement and the houses of the rich, God of the subway and the night club, God of the cathedral and the streets, God of the sober and the drunk, the junkie and the stripper, the gambler and the good family man; dear God, help us to see the world and its children through your eyes, and to love accordingly.

Monica Furlong

O Lord God our Father, we beseech you guide those who bear authority in our towns and cities, that there may be noble streets and open ways therein, that all the skill and beauty of art and craft may be drawn into the service of the common people, for your glory and the delight of men. Give them inspiration and courage, O Lord, to sweep away all mean streets and unworthy habitations, that men and women may be finely bred and taught and trained, and that your Kingdom may come on earth, for Christ's sake.

The Challenge

12

TRAVEL

Grant me a steady hand and watchful eye
that no man shall be hurt when I pass by.
Thou gavest life, and I pray no act of mine
may take away or mar that gift of Thine.
Shelter those, dear Lord, who bear me company
from the evils of fire and all calamity.
Teach me to use my car for others' need,
nor miss through love of speed
the beauties of Thy world; that thus I may
with joy and courtesy go on my way.

The Motorist's Prayer

O Loving Father, we remember before thee all those who travel or whose work calls them to the distant places of the earth: in loneliness may they be helped by the knowledge that others are remembering them; in time of temptation may they be given strength to hold fast to what they know to be right: and may the sense of thy presence and the knowledge of thy fatherly love be ever with them. Through Jesus Christ our Lord.   AMEN

> May the road rise to meet you.
> May the wind be always at your back.
> May the sun shine warm upon your face,
> the rains fall soft upon your fields and,
> until we meet again,
> may God hold you in the palm of his hand.
>
> An Irish Blessing

If a person is at times to draw close to the Divine, then under normal conditions he must be neither divine nor anything approaching it.

Yukio Mishima 1925–70

Thou hast set my feet in a large room.

Psalm 31:8

LEISURE

Slow me down, Lord! Ease the pounding of my heart by the quietening of my mind. Steady my hurried pace with a vision of the eternal reach of time. Give me the calmness of the everlasting hills. Break the tensions of my nerves and muscles with the soothing music of the singing streams. Help me to know the magical, restoring power of sleep.

Teach me the art of taking minute vacations . . . of slowing down to look at a flower, to chat with a friend, to pat the dog, to read a few lines from a good book. Remind me each day of the fable of the hare and the tortoise, that I may know that the race is not always to the swift; that there is more to life than measuring its speed.

Let me look upwards into the branches of the towering oak and know that it grew great and strong because it grew slowly and well. Slow me down, Lord, and inspire me to send my roots deep into the soil of life's enduring values that I may grow towards the star of my greater destiny. AMEN

Lord, of all good life, we thank you for leisure which gives us space to enjoy beauty of thought and sound and sight in our busy, driven world. We thank you for the enrichment given to us through art and literature, music and dancing, for the satisfying search after beauty in the common things of every day, in our furniture, our cups and saucers, our clothes, our handicrafts, our gardens. We thank you that you have given us both our pleasures and the capacity to enjoy them. Keep us generous in our enjoyment and save us from all forms of selfishness which keep us in bondage instead of setting us free to live fully in our leisure as well as in our work.

We ask it for your name's sake. AMEN

There is no better armour against sin than joy.

Elizabeth Goudge

NATIONS

Lover of all men, widen the bounds of our caring and our serving by the influence of your sovereign friendship. May your generous love break down our defences, our prejudices, our dislikes, that in our everyday contacts with people and in all our thoughts of men of other nations and races, we may show forth your gentleness and courtesy, your sympathy and friendliness. To the honour and glory of the loving Father of all.   AMEN

With malice towards none; with charity for all; with firmness in the right as God gives us to see the right, let us strive on to finish the work we are in: to bind up the nation's wounds; to care for him who shall have borne the battle and for his widow and orphan – to do all which may achieve and cherish a just and lasting peace among ourselves and with all nations.

Abraham Lincoln 1809–65

My country is the world, and my religion is to do good.

Thomas Paine 1737–1809

Grant, O Lord,
   that we may approach every question of foreign policy from the point of sight of our creed;
   that we may check in ourselves and in others every temper which makes for war, all ungenerous judgements, all presumptuous claims, all promptings of self-assertion, the growth of ignorance and passion;
   that we may endeavour to understand the needs, the feelings, the endowments, the traditional aspirations of other countries;
   that we may do gladly, unweariedly, patiently, what lies in us to remove suspicions and misunderstandings; that we may honour all men.   AMEN

Bishop Westcott 1825–1901

We pray, Father of all, who loves all men, for a new Britain, a new Europe, a new America, a new Asia, and a new world, wherein every race may be free, and government may be of the people, by all and for all, so that the nations, ordering their states wisely and worthily, may live in the example of your Son Jesus Christ our Lord, to whom with the Father and the Holy Spirit, may all the praise of the world be given, all power, dominion and glory for ever.   AMEN

We pray for our Land. Raise up nobler men – men that shall scorn bribes; men that shall not run greedily to ambition; men that shall not be devoured by selfishness; men that fear God and love man; men that shall love this country with a pure and disinterested love. And so we beseech Thee that our peace may stand firm upon integrity, and that righteousness may everywhere prevail.   AMEN

Father, you have made all men in your likeness and love all whom you have made. Suffer not our family to separate itself from you by building barriers of race and colour. As your son our Saviour was born of a Hebrew Mother, but rejoiced in the faith of a Syrian woman and of a Roman soldier, welcomed the Greeks who sought him, and suffered an African to carry his cross, so teach us to regard the members of all races as fellow heirs of the Kingdom of Jesus Christ our Lord.   AMEN

15

CHURCH

O God, our Shepherd give to the Church a new vision and a new charity, new wisdom and fresh understanding, the revival of her brightness and the renewal of her unity; that the eternal message of Thy Son, undefiled by the traditions of men, may be hailed as the good news of the new age; through him who maketh all things new, Jesus Christ our Lord. AMEN

Percy Dearmer 1867–1936

O God of unchangeable power and eternal light, look favourably on your whole Church, that wonderful and sacred mystery, and carry out the work of man's salvation; and let the whole world feel and see that things which were cast down are being raised up, and things which had grown old are being made new, and all things are returning to perfection, through Jesus Christ our Lord. AMEN

From the *Gelasian Sacramentary*:
used in Series 2 Holy Communion

When in sorrow, read John 14.
When men fail you, read Psalm 27.
When you have sinned, read Psalm 51.
When you worry, read Matthew 6:19–34.
Before Church service, read Psalm 84.
When you are in danger, read Psalm 91.
When you have the blues, read Psalm 139.
When you are discouraged, read Isaiah 40.
If you want to be fruitful, read John 15.
When doubts come upon you, try John 7:17.
When you are lonely or fearful, read Psalm 23.
When you forget your blessings, read Psalm 103.
For Jesus' idea of a Christian, read Matthew 5.
For James' idea of religion, read James 1:19–27.

When your faith needs stirring, read Hebrews 11.
When you feel down and out, read Romans 8:31-39.
When you want courage for your task, read Joshua 1.
When the world seems bigger than God, read Psalm 90.
When you want rest and peace, read Matthew 11:28-30.
When you want Christian assurance, read Romans 8:1-30.
For Paul's secret of happiness, read Colossians 3:12-17.
When you leave home for labour or travel, read Psalm 121.
When you grow bitter or critical, read 1 Corinthians 13.
When your prayers grow narrow or selfish, read Psalm 67.
For Paul's rules on how to get along with men, read Romans 12.
When you think of investments and returns, read Mark 10:17-31.
For a great invitation and a great opportunity, read Isaiah 55.
For Jesus' idea of prayer, read Luke 11:1-13; Matthew 6:5-15.
Why not follow Psalm 119:11 and hide some of these in your
memory?

How to Use the Bible

NOON

The day becomes more solemn and serene
when noon is passed.

Shelley

I

CREED

The living Christ still has two hands,
one to point the way,
and the other held out to help us along.

T. W. Mason

A creed is a rod
and a crown is of night;
And this thing is of God:
to be man with thy might,
to grow straight in the strength of the Spirit
and live out thy life as THE LIGHT.

A. C. Swinburne 1837-1909

Thou takest the pen – and the lines dance.
Thou takest the flute – and the notes shimmer.
Thou takest the brush – and the colours sing.
So all things have meaning and beauty in that space beyond time
where Thou art. How, then, can I hold back anything from Thee?

Dag Hammarskjold 1905-61, *Markings*

Eternal God and Father, by whose power we are created and by whose
love we are redeemed: guide and strengthen us by thy Spirit, that
we may give ourselves to thy service, and live this day in love to one
another and to thee; through Jesus Christ thy Son our Lord. AMEN

Morning Prayer, Series 2 Revised

Let there be peace on the earth,
And let it begin with me.

He is the Way.
Follow Him through the Land of Unlikeness:
You will see rare beasts and have unique adventures.
He is the Truth.
Seek Him in the Kingdom of Anxiety;
You will come to a great city that has expected your return for years.
He is the Life.
Love Him in the World of the Flesh;
And at your marriage all its occasions shall dance for joy.

W. H. Auden 1907–1973

To be sincere is to direct one's attention towards God, to remember Him, attain to Him, cut oneself off from all that is other than God. This, in fact, is the goal of all worship.

Aqa Jamal Khwansari 18th century

I will try to discover some new beauty, some new sound or sight or thought that I have never heard nor seen nor contemplated. I will try to show my appreciation for this gift of beauty by giving in return some part of myself. I will make some small part of this world a little better than it was, and this undertaking may be so grand as the planting of a tree or so small as the picking up of a scrap of paper on the street.

I will not turn away from ugliness, in my environment or in the people with whom I share this earth. Sometimes in ugliness there is beauty hidden, and where there is not, it lies within my power to make the ugly a little less so.

And so I will not respond to the hostility of man – or nature – with anger or vindictiveness. I will turn away ill-temper with a smile and chide only myself for not carrying an umbrella when it rains. Our years on this planet are brief enough. Let it be said of me when I am gone: 'He gave as much or more than he got. He may not have found beauty every day of his life, *but he looked for it every day of his life.*'

W. B. Prescott

Sow a thought and you reap a deed,
sow a deed and you reap a habit,
sow a habit and you reap a character,
sow a character and you reap a destiny.

Charles Reade 1814–64

The religion of Sydney Smith – Never let a day pass without doing a
kindness to somebody.

2

FAITH

A faith fit to live by.
A self fit to live with.
A work fit to live for.
Somebody to love and be loved by.
These make life.

Susan Stone

Lord, I say nothing: I profess
no faith in Thee nor Christ Thy Son:
Yet no man ever heard me mock
a true believing one.

If knowledge is not great enough
to give a man believing power,
Lord, he must wait in Thy great hand
till revelation's hour.

Meanwhile he'll follow Christ the man,
in that humanity he taught,
which to the poor and the oppressed
gives its best time and thought.

Short Prayers for the Long Day

Jesus, confirm my heart's desire
to work, and speak, and think for thee;
Still let me guard the holy fire
and still stir up the gift in me.

Still let me prove thy perfect will,
my acts of faith and love repeat,
till death thy endless mercies seal
and make the sacrifice complete.

Charles Wesley 1707–88

Thou shalt know him when he comes,
not by any din of drums –
nor the vantage of airs –
nor by anything he wears.
Neither by his crown –
nor his gown.
For his presence known shall be
by the holy harmony
that his coming makes in thee.

15th century

Stone by stone a wall is built,
and each stone must lie square.
Little by little a rose unfolds,
and each petal must be fair.
Little by little faith is built,
and day by day it grows.
Stronger at last than a wall of stone
and lovelier than a rose.

CHRISTIAN HALLMARK

Lord Jesus Christ,
you have told us in no uncertain terms
what is expected of us
when we
say we love you.

You have made it clear
that if we want to serve you,
express our love for you
and give joy to God,
that we shall do it
in our neighbours
wherever we find them,
by meeting their needs.
We will find you in Church
and in the streets;
We will find you
on the bus
and in the train;
we will find you
in the office and the shop,
in the hospital ward,
in prison,
in places
where we would never think to go.

For every foolish word,
every malicious thought,
and every godless act,
every neglect of human need,
every arrogant assertion
of our own goodness,
Lord,

forgive us.
So work in us
that each of us
in our own small way
may be a refuge,
a refreshment
and a sure support
for the anxious,
the weary
and the weak;
in the name of Jesus Christ our Lord.

Alan Gaunt

O Lord Jesus, acknowledge what is thine in us, and take away from us all that is not thine; for thy honour and glory.   AMEN

St Bernardine 1388–1444

Christians are not distinguished from the rest of mankind either in locality or speech or custom. For they dwell not somewhere in cities of their own, neither do they use some different language, nor practise an extraordinary kind of rite. But while they dwell in the cities of Greeks and Barbarians as the lot of each is cast, and follow the native customs in dress and food and the other arrangements of life, yet the constitution of their own citizenship, which they set forth, is marvellous and confessedly contradicts expectations. They dwell in their own countries, but only as sojourners: they bear their share in all things as citizens and they endure all hardship as strangers. Every foreign country is a father-land to them and every father-land is foreign. They obey the established laws, and they surpass the laws in their own lives. In a word, what a soul is in a body, this the Christians are in the world.

From the anonymous *Epistle to Diognetus*

Was Christ a man like us? Ah! Let us try
If we then, too, can be such men as He.

Matthew Arnold 1822–88

4

GUIDANCE

O Lord Jesus Christ, who art the Way, the Truth and the Life, we pray thee suffer us not to stray from thee who art the Way, nor to distrust thee who art the Truth, nor to rest in any other thing than thee, who art the Life. Teach us by thy Holy Spirit what to believe, what to do and wherein to take our rest. AMEN

Erasmus 1466–1536

Grant, O God, we beseech you,
that the same mind be in all of us,
that was in Christ Jesus:
his self-forgetting, humility,
    interest in common things,
his love for common people,
    compassion for the fallen,
his tolerance with the mistaken,
his patience with the slow,
and in our work make us continually
sensitive to your guidance
and ready for your will,
through Jesus Christ our Lord. AMEN

Lord Jesus Christ, who alone art Wisdom, Thou knowest what is best for us; mercifully grant that it may happen to us only as it is pleasing to Thee and as seems good in Thy sight this day; for Thy Name's sake. AMEN

Henry VI 1421–61

5
LOVE

i *Freedom*

God speaks:
When you love someone you love him as he is.
I alone am perfect.
It is probably for that reason
that I know what perfection is
and that I demand less perfection of those poor people.

I know how difficult it is.
And how often when they are struggling in their trials,
how often do I wish and am tempted to put my hand under their
    stomachs,
in order to hold them up with my big hand,
just like a father teaching his son how to swim,
in the current of the river . . .

Such is the mystery of man's freedom, says God,
and the mystery of my government towards him and towards his
    freedom.
If I hold him up too much, he is no longer free,
and if I don't hold him up sufficiently, I am endangering his salvation.
Two goods in a sense almost equally precious,
for salvation is of infinite price . . .
Because I myself am free, says God, and I have created man in my
    own image and likeness.
Such is the mystery, such is the secret, such is the price of all freedom.

Charles Péguy 1873-1914

From the rising of the sun unto the going down of the same,
of thy Goodness give us,
by thy Love inspire us,
by thy Spirit guide us,
by thy Power protect us
and in thy Mercy receive us
now and always.   AMEN

O Lord, help us, now and always, to listen for the voice of God,
to think fairly,
to love widely,
to witness humbly,
to build bravely.

Toc H Prayer

Grant us, O Lord, the royalty of inward happiness, and the serenity which comes from living close to thee. Daily renew in us the sense of joy, and let the eternal spirit dwell in our souls and bodies, filling every corner of our hearts with light and gladness; so that, bearing about with us the infection of a good courage, we may be diffusers of life, and meet all that comes, of good or evil, even death itself, with gallant and high-hearted happiness; giving thee thanks always for all things. Through Jesus Christ our Lord.   AMEN

Toc H Prayer

Love is God's Holy of Holies.
Love alone is salvation.
Only in the Temple of Love do I worship God.

Love alone introduces God to us.
Where Love is, there God is.

Toyohiko Kagawa 1888-1960

1. Make up your mind to be happy. Learn to find pleasure in simple things.

2. Make the best of your circumstances. No one has everything and everyone has something of sorrow intermingled with the gladness of life. The trick is to make the laughter outweigh the tears.

3. Don't take yourself too seriously. Don't think that somehow you should be protected from misfortunes that befall others.

4. You can't please everybody. Don't let criticism worry you.

5. Don't let your neighbour set your standards. Be yourself.

6. Do the things you enjoy doing, but stay out of debt.

7. Don't borrow trouble. Imaginary things are harder to bear than the actual ones.

8. Since hate poisons the soul, do not cherish enmities, grudges. Avoid people who make you unhappy.

9. Have many interests. If you can't travel, read about new places.

10. Don't hold post-mortems. Don't spend your life brooding over sorrows and mistakes. Don't be one who never gets over things.

11. Do what you can for those less fortunate than yourself.

12. Keep busy at something. A very busy person never has time to be unhappy.

Robert Louis Stevenson 1850–94, *A Pattern for Living*

ii *Universality*

All men look at you, Lord,
all men love your eyes;
for in them they see
the fire, and love that never dies.

They look and they see in you
all that they need to be,
and as much of the love of God
as eyes can hope to see.

Noon: Love

And still you beckon onward
with a love that never dies:
yet all we have to do, Lord,
is see it in your eyes.

Giles Harcourt 1936–

Remember the faith that took men from home
at the call of a wandering preacher.
Our age is an age of moderate virtue . . .
When men will not lay down the Cross
because they will assume it.
Yet nothing is impossible, nothing,
To men of faith and conviction.
Let us therefore make perfect our will.
O God, help us.

T. S. Eliot 1888–1965

Lord:
How do I love thee? Let me count the ways.
I love thee to the depth and breadth and height
my soul can reach, when feeling out of sight
for the ends of being and of ideal grace.
I love thee to the level of every day's
most quiet need, by sun and candlelight.
I love thee freely, as men strive for right;
I love thee purely, as they turn from praise.
I love thee with a passion put to use
in my old griefs, and with my childhood faith.
I love thee with a love I seemed to lose
with my lost saints – I love thee with the breath,
smiles, tears, of all my life!
And, God, if thou dost choose
I shall love thee better after death.

Elizabeth Browning (adapted) 1806–61

O merciful Father, who has made of one blood all nations of men; grant us a universal love towards all men. Give to us such a tenderness of heart that we may feel deeply the miseries and calamities of our brethren, and diligently remember them in love. Grant that we may not only seek our own things, but also the things of others. Let this mind be also in us which was in Christ Jesus, that we may love as brethren, that we may be pitiful and courteous, and may endeavour heartily and vigorously to keep the unity of the spirit in the bond of peace; and may the God of grace, mercy and peace be with us all.

Thomas à Kempis 1379–1471

The love of which I speak is slow to lose patience – it looks for a way of being constructive. It is not possessive: it is neither anxious to impress, nor does it cherish inflated ideas of its own importance.

Love has good manners and does not pursue self advantage. It is not touchy. It does not keep account of evil or gloat over the wickedness of other people. On the contrary it is glad with all good men when truth prevails.

Love knows no limit to its endurance, no end to its trust, no fading of its hope: it can outlast anything. It is, in fact, the one good thing that still stands when all else has fallen.

from I Corinthians 13 (J. B. Phillips translation)

iii *Unselfishness*

Help me to love, Lord
not to waste my powers of love,
to love myself less and less in order to love others more and more,
that around me, no one should suffer or die because I have stolen the
   love they needed to live.

Michel Quoist 1918–

Noon: Love

O God,
who gives men strength
grant them also gentleness.
To those you have endowed with talent
confer, too, the consoling gift of understanding.
To the perceptive give the quality of sympathy;
to the righteous an unerring instinct for mercy;
to the proud a sense of their own insignificance;
to the arrogant the white crown of humility.
And to those who feel over-secure amid all man's achievements
a befitting awareness of life's transience.

Dear Lord,
gather our various strengths and weaknesses
and touch them with the radiance of your love,
so that men, sharing each others' joys and burdens,
may walk steadfastly toward the gates of achievement
beyond which lies the heaven of your creation.

Melville Harcourt 1909–

The six most important words in the world:
I ADMIT I MADE A MISTAKE.
The five most important words in the world:
YOU DID A GOOD JOB.
The four most important words in the world:
WHAT IS YOUR OPINION?
The three most important words in the world:
IF YOU PLEASE.
The two most important words in the world:
THANK YOU.
The most important word in the world:
WE.
The least important word in the world:
I.

Self is the only prison that can ever bind the soul;
Love is the only angel who can bid the gates unroll;
And when he comes and calls thee, arise and follow fast,
His way may lead through darkness but it leads to life at last.

Henry van Dyke

iv *Tolerance*

The girl kept pressing her cheek against the man's shoulder with great tenderness. He only yawned. She gave: he took without visible response. Were they equal in loving? For equality in loving is rare and this is why love is so closely linked to pain. Rare, too, is it for Christ's love to be returned with fierce intensity.

Roger Bush, Prayers for Pagans

He staggered down the steps and fell, Lord,
a crumpled mass on the footpath.
His bottle broke and liquid spilled across the walk.
He's drunk, I thought. Disgust. Disdain. Until . . .
two girls rushed from a nearby car and cried:
'It's Daddy. Please help. He's ill.'

10/88

11/88

Roger Bush, Prayers for Pagans

He caught my gaze. This greedy-eyed young man.
He too had seen the open handbag on the aged arm,
with the few dollars exposed to view.
He stalked his prey, and the old woman just window-shopped.
He'll grab and run, I thought. But no.
Quietly he tapped her shoulder, pointed to the bag, exchanged smiles.
They went their way.
O Lord, forgive me; forgive me.
Why do I always think the worst of your children?

Roger Bush, Prayers for Pagans

Noon: Love

We are your offspring
and wish to love you
in ways that are best:
not with foolishness,
but with care for others;
not with selfishness,
but with love of our brothers
who know only the bitterness
of prejudice and the hate of racial pride,
who live in the earth's lonely places
knowing not the love of friends
nor the laughter of carefree hearts.
Help us, dear Lord, to remember
those who know not health,
and cannot give joy
because they live with pain.
Help us too, dear Christ,
to remember with gratitude
the blessings we so often forget;
the air we breathe, the food we eat,
the friends we have;
But, above all,
the joy we can give to others
by kindness,
thoughtfulness
and courtesy,
a ready smile
and a cheerful manner.
From the example of him
who gave the very best he had,
more and more every day,
our friend and guide,
our comfort and support,
even Christ, your Son, our Lord.   AMEN
                                   Giles Harcourt 1936–

A man who desires to help others by counsel or deed will refrain from dwelling on men's faults, and will speak but sparingly of human weaknesses.

Baruch Spinoza 1632-77

Lord, thou knowest better than I know myself that I am growing
    older and will some day be old.
Keep me from the fatal habit of thinking I must say something on
    Every subject and on every occasion.
Release me from craving to straighten out everybody's affairs.
Make me thoughtful but not moody; helpful but not bossy.
With my vast store of wisdom, it seems a pity not to use it all,
but thou knowest, Lord, that I want a few friends at the end.
Keep my mind free from the recital of endless details;
give me wings to get to the point.
Seal my lips on my aches and pains:
They are increasing, and the love of rehearsing them is becoming
    sweeter as the years go by.
I dare not ask for grace enough to enjoy the tales of other's pains,
but help me endure them with patience.
I dare not ask for improved memory, but for a growing humility,
and a lessening cock-sureness when my memory seems to clash with
    the memory of others.
Teach me the glorious lesson that occasionally I may be mistaken.
Keep me reasonably sweet; I do not want to be a saint . . .
some of them are so hard to live with . . .
but a sour old person is one of the crowning works of the Devil.
Give me the ability to see good things in unexpected places,
and talents in unexpected people.
And give me, O Lord, the grace to tell them so.   AMEN

Dear Lord, I have few gifts and not many opportunities, as I see it, to express my faith in a generation that grabs all the advertising space for secular success, whether it's money, possessions, or mere social acclaim. As a custodian of your truth may I, in this topsy-turvy world, strive each day to live out my personal faith in terms of courage, unselfishness, humour, understanding and tolerance, especially during those twilight hours when, whether alone or with others, I find day-to-day living most difficult. In this way perhaps, I can get nearer to you and closer and more sympathetic to those whose worthiness I sometimes find it hard to recognize. I ask this in your Name who, through sheer love of mankind, endured the Cross.
AMEN

Melville Harcourt 1909-

Slow to suspect – quick to trust,
Slow to condemn – quick to justify,
Slow to offend – quick to defend,
Slow to expose – quick to shield,
Slow to reprimand – quick to forebear.
Slow to belittle – quick to appreciate,
Slow to demand – quick to serve,
Slow to provoke – quick to conciliate,
Slow to hinder – quick to help,
Slow to resent – quick to forgive.

v Friendship

Almighty and most merciful Father, who has given us a new commandment that we should love one another, give us also grace that we may fulfil it. Make us gentle, courteous, and forbearing. Direct our lives so that we may look each to the good of others in word and deed. And hallow all our friendships by the blessing of thy spirit, for his sake, who loveth us and gave himself for us, Jesus Christ our Lord.
AMEN

Bishop Westcott 1825-1901

Short Prayers for the Long Day

Life needs
> security and hope

security being
the fundamental basis
> the earth
> > in which life is born.

Hope being
that call . . . to light
> and love
> > and beauty
> . . . universality
> shadows of the infinite
> risk
> and hope

love of the unknown
passionate interest in the present

thirst for adventure
desire for new experiences

outpourings of generosity
quest for knowledge
openness to the future
call to love
availability to the Spirit
peaceful contemplation
> high skies
> mountains
> deep lakes
> deep breathing
> wonderment

Love is the greatest of all risks

> the giving of myself

but do I dare take this risk

Noon: Love

diving into the cool
   swirling
   living waters of
    LOVING FIDELITY.

Jean Vanier 1916-

May I be no man's enemy, and may I be the friend of that which is eternal and abides.

May I never quarrel with those nearest me: and if I do, may I be reconciled quickly.

May I love, seek, and attain only that which is good.

May I wish for all men's happiness and envy none.

May I never rejoice in the ill-fortune of one who has wronged me.

When I have done or said what is wrong, may I never wait for the rebuke of others, but always rebuke myself until I make amends.

May I win no victory that harms either me or my opponent.

May I reconcile friends who are angry with one another.

May I, to the extent of my power, give all needful help to my friends and all who are in want.

May I never fail a friend who is in danger.

When visiting those in grief may I be able by gentle and healing words to soften their pain.

May I respect myself.

May I always keep tame that which rages within me.

May I accustom myself to be gentle, and never be angry with people because of circumstances.

May I never discuss who is wicked and what wicked things he has done, but know good men and follow in their footsteps.

Eusebius 3rd century

A faithful friend is a secure shelter;
whoever finds one has found a treasure.
A faithful friend is beyond price;
his worth is more than money can buy.
A faithful friend is an elixir of life,
found only by those who fear the Lord.
The man who fears the Lord keeps his friendships in repair,
for he treats his neighbour as himself.

Ecclesiasticus 6:7 (NEB)

O God of love, we pray you give us love: love in our thinking, love in our speaking, love in our doing and love in the hidden places of our souls; love of our neighbours, near and far; love of our friends, old and new; love of those with whom we find it hard to bear, and love of those who find it hard to bear with us; love of those with whom we work, and love of those with whom we take our ease; love in joy, love in sorrow, love in life, and love in death, so that at length we may be worthy to dwell with you, who are Eternal Love.

6

THE CALLING

i *Dedication*

Bless, O God, all who dedicate their powers today to the making of peace in the world;

Bless all who give their training and experience to feed and clothe and house the destitute:

Bless all who lend their energies and skills to teach impoverished people to till their land, to water it, and harvest it.

And give us all a lively concern for the underprivileged, and show us practical ways of helping. For Christ's sake.   AMEN

Rita Snowden

Let us Renew the Sense of our Vocation in Jesus Christ
Reminding ourselves again:

that we are not our own: we are bought with a price.

That we did not choose Christ: he chose us and ordained us to bear fruit.

That he gave us an example as now he gives us his Spirit, that we may follow his steps.

Let us Review our Relations with Others
If, being busy and absorbed, we have failed in companionship and understanding towards other members of the family, counting their lives less important than our own; if we offer our best to those outside, but fail in joyfulness and fall victims to routine at home.

Let us seek earnestly that the love of God may be shed abroad in our hearts.

Student Book of Prayers

Listen now, whoever you may be,
if your soul is lit by the love of God:
you cannot leave this world all by yourself,
set out on the great path with empty hands,
arrive before the Gates of God – which your faith dreams
stand underneath the arch of the Eternal Home –
to say 'Lord, Lord, I have brought nothing with me;
give me a place in the love of your divine light.'

Because the Lord your God will answer 'Go.
Hack up your feet on red unending ice,
lean on the knotted stick of all your hatreds;
and you shall be a wanderer eternally unless
you find the palm of love which you refused to take
from the tree which was seeded by my blood.'

Marcos Ana
[A political prisoner who was in Burgos Jail
for twenty-two years. Translated by
Chloe Valliamy and Stephen Sodley]

O Blessed Lord Jesus Christ, who bade your disciples stand with their loins girt and their lamps burning, be with us at this hour. Here we dedicate ourselves to you. Help us to gird up our loins to run the race that is set before us with redoubled vigour and fresh vision. Teach us how to trim our lamps that they may not burn dim. Guide us to the constant recollection that the candle of the Lord is the spirit of man. And by your risen power make us a power in this place, for your sake. AMEN

I bind unto myself today
the power of God to hold and lead;
his eye to watch, his might to stay,
his ear to hearken to my need;
the wisdom of my God to teach,
his hand to guide, his shield to ward,
the word of God to give me speech,
his heavenly host to be my guard.

attributed to St Patrick 372–466

O Lord Jesus Christ,
take as your right,
receive as my gift,
all my liberty,
my memory, my understanding, my will,
all that I have
all that I am
all that I can be.
To you, O Lord, I restore it,
all is yours,
dispose of it according to your will.
Give me your love.
Give me your grace.
It is enough for me.

St Ignatius 1491–1556

Noon: Calling

My God, I offer Thee
all Thou appointest me;
all that the day may bring
of joy or suffering;
all that Thou givest today;
all that Thou takest away;
all Thou would'st have me be;
My God, I offer Thee.

ii *Channelling*

Lord, make me a channel of your peace,
that where there is hatred I may bring love;
that where there is wrong I may bring the spirit of forgiveness;
that where there is discord I may bring harmony;
that where there is error I may bring truth;
that where there is doubt I may bring faith;
that where there is despair I may bring hope;
that where there are shadows I may bring your light;
and where there is sadness I may bring joy.
Lord grant that I may seek rather to comfort than to be comforted,
to understand than to be understood,
to love than to be loved:
for it is by giving that one receives,
it is by self-forgetting that one finds,
it is by forgiving that one is forgiven,
it is by dying that one awakens to eternal life.

St Francis of Assisi 1181–1226

Two men please God –
he who serves him with all his heart
because he knows him.
he who seeks him with all his heart
because he knows him not.

Short Prayers for the Long Day

Lord, when I look at life
may I see through your eyes,
sensitively.

Lord, when I hear men speak
may I listen with your ears,
attentively.

Lord, when I speak to men
may I use your words,
thoughtfully.

Lord, when I use my hands
may I give your hands,
caringly.

Lord, as I live each day
may I walk with you,
lovingly.

Giles Harcourt 1936–

He that is down need fear no fall,
he that is low, no pride;
he that is humble ever shall
have God to be his Guide.

I am content with what I have,
little be it or much:
And, Lord, contentment still I crave,
because thou savest such.

Fulness to such a burden is
that go on pilgrimage:
Here little, and hereafter bliss,
is best from age to age.

John Bunyan 1628–88

O God
  my God
    keep me from flinching/waning
        slumbering into that timeless rest
        that never is
keep me from falling into a prison
        of egotistical habits
          where the bars
          are superficial friends
            and drinks
            and stupid laughter
            kisses without love
            business and organization
              without heart
            and gifts for self-flattery
        these bars that prevent life evolving
          towards that taste of the infinite
          open to your call . . .
  break down those barriers
      that prevent me living, my God.

Jean Vanier 1916–

Jesus said: Not every one that saith unto me, Lord, Lord, shall enter into the kingdom of heaven; but he that doeth the will of my Father who is in heaven. Whosoever shall do the will of God, the same is my brother and sister.

It is the will of God that we should endeavour to keep our bodies in health and strength, and our appetites and impulses under control, and everywhere and in all things to be temperate and pure.

Grant to us, Lord, we beseech thee, the spirit to think and do always such things as be rightful; that we, who cannot do anything that is good without thee, may, by thee, be enabled to live according to thy will; through Jesus Christ our Lord.　AMEN

Student Book of Prayers

Short Prayers for the Long Day

This is our poverty –
that we do not belong to each other
nor serve one another.
We go each his own way
and do not care for our neighbour.
We pray thee, O Lord
redeem us from this estrangement.
Redeem us out of this loneliness.
Deliver us from the sin that divides us.
Join us closely in True Love.

> The Church in Germany

Where there is hatred
or hunger,
where there is guilt
and despair,
where there is war
and misery;
where there is hunger
and illness;
where men and women laugh,
and where they cry,
where they are glad,
or sad,
help us to find you, Lord,
and serve you;
help us to bring you to the fullness of life
in God's little ones

> Alan Gaunt

iii *Giving*

Two mites, two drops (yet all her house and land),
falls from a steady heart, though trembling hand.
The other's wanton wealth foams high and brave,
The other cast away, she only gave.

Richard Crashaw 1613-49
'The Widow's Mite'

And you God
for whom I make my way in this immense sky
along clouds of worlds
you are lonelier, poorer than I,
in order to live I must be brother to you,
and father,
and wipe your dripping nose,
support your failing steps,
build you a strong house of stone
solid and upright, and restore you
when your helpless forehead
burns on my knees;
and get bread for you, soup,
and the honey and fruit which please you.
This is my worship.

Danilo Dolci 1924-

No sacrifice is worth the name unless it is a joy.
Sacrifice and a long face go ill together.

Mahatma Gandhi 1868-1948

What does the Lord require of you
but to do justly
to love mercy
and to walk humbly with your God.

Micah 6:8

Then shall the King say unto them on his right hand,
Come, ye blessed of my Father, inherit the Kingdom
prepared for you from the foundation of the world;
For I was an hungered, and ye gave me meat;
I was thirsty, and ye gave me drink;
I was a stranger, and ye took me in;
Naked, and ye clothed me;
I was sick, and ye visited me;
I was in prison, and ye came unto me.

Matthew 25:34-7 (AV)

iv *Service*

O Lord, renew our spirits and draw our hearts unto thyself, that our work may not be to us a burden, but a delight; and give us such a mighty love to thee as may sweeten all our obedience. O, let us not serve thee with the spirit of bondage as slaves but with the cheerfulness and gladness of children, delighting ourselves in thee and rejoicing in thy work.   AMEN

Benjamin Jenks 1646

I should give everything,
I should give everything till there is not a single pain,
a single misery, a single sin in the world.
I should then give all, Lord, all the time.
I should give my life.

Lord, it is not true, is it?
It is not true for everyone?
I am exaggerating, I must be sensible!

Son, there is only *one* commandment, for Everyone:
You shall love with *all* your heart,
          with *all* your soul,
          with *all* your strength.

Michel Quoist 1918–

Teach us, good Lord, to serve thee as thou deservest; to give and not to count the cost; to fight and not to heed the wounds; to toil and not to seek for rest; to labour and not to ask for any reward, save that of knowing that we do thy will, through the same Jesus Christ our Lord. AMEN

St Ignatius 1491–1556

This is my prayer to thee, my lord;
Give me the strength lightly to bear my joys and sorrows;
Give me the strength to make my love fruitful in service;
Give me the strength never to disown the poor or bend my knees
    before insolent might.
Give me the strength to raise my mind high above daily trifles.
And give me the strength to surrender my strength to thy will with
    love.

Rabindranath Tagore 1861–1941

O Lord Jesus Christ, we thank you for your great example of love and service to all whom you met in your life on earth. We thank you for giving us life with all its powers. Help us to learn that the best use for our gifts is in service to you and our fellow men. Help us to see all people as you see them, and to be ready to give our lives to the service of others. AMEN

E. M. Venables

Help us, O Lord, to work together for the good of one another. Give us courage to do our part worthily; to maintain unfalteringly the ideals of love and service that we have learnt of Christ; to accept no standard of honesty, purity and truth but that which he has taught; and so to work and pray that when our days here shall end we may know that we have striven not in vain to uphold what is right, to be worthy of our trust, to be of service to our fellow men and thee.
AMEN

E. M. Venables

Father, give us grace not to pass by suffering or joy without eyes to see; give us understanding and sympathy, and guard us from clumsiness, that we may in our hearts be sorry with those who weep and be glad with those who rejoice. Use us, if it be possible to make happy and strong the hearts of others and humbly to set forth your light which is the Light of the World; through Jesus Christ our Lord. AMEN

O God, from whom to be turned is to fall,
to whom to be turned is to rise,
and in whom to stand is to abide for ever;
grant to all in adversity your help,
to all in perplexity your guidance,
to all in danger your protection,
to all in sorrow your peace;
through Jesus Christ, our Lord.

St Augustine 354–430
(adapted by N. Goodacre)

As thou, Lord, hast lived for others
so may we for others live;
freely have thy gifts been granted,
freely may thy servants give.
Thine the gold and thine the silver,
thine the wealth of land and sea,
we but stewards of thy bounty,
held in solemn trust for thee.

S. C. Lowry 1855–1932

O Lord, we pray that you will hasten the time when no man shall live in contentment while he knows that his neighbour has need. Inspire in us and in all men the consciousness that we are not our own but yours and our neighbours; for his sake, who prayed that we might all be one in him – Christ Jesus our Lord. AMEN

For joys of service, thee we praise,
whose favour crowneth all our days;
For humble tasks that bring delight,
when done, O Lord, as in thy sight.
Accept our offerings, Lord most high,
our work, our purpose sanctify,
and with our gifts may we have place,
now in the Kingdom of thy grace.

St Venantius 530–609

O God, it is easy to love the whole world, but hard to love the person one works next to;

O God, it is easy to campaign for world peace, but hard to contribute to the peace within my own home;

O God, it is easy to be fascinated with some new truth, and miss you in the thing I have known so long;

O God, it is easy to share my home, and possessions with people I like. Teach me how to be generous towards others.

Enable me today to say something, or do something that will make a difference
    to the discouraged,
    to the inexperienced,
    to the despairing.

Let no selfish concern with my own affairs, shut me off from any today. For your love's sake.   AMEN

Rita Snowden

v *Courage*

The Lord is the strength of my life: of whom then shall I be afraid?

Psalm 27:1

O God, give me the strength
to look up and not down,
to look forward and not back,
to look out and not in, and
to lend a hand.

Edward Everett Hale

All-loving Father, may this be a time of unclouded vision and deep resolution. To this end make us ready. Grant grace that many more may find the way, and walk in it with faith and hope and courage; through Jesus Christ our Saviour.   AMEN

You, who are heroic love, keep alive in our hearts that adventurous spirit which makes men scorn the way of safety, so that your will may be done. For only thus, Lord, shall we be worthy of those courageous souls who in every age have ventured all in obedience to your call, and for whom the trumpets sounded on the other side. Through Jesus Christ our Lord.   AMEN

Toc H Prayer

Grant us, Lord, grace to follow wheresoever you go. In little daily duties to which you call us, bow down our wills to simple obedience, patience, strict truthfulness of word and manner, humility and kindness. In great acts of duty, if you should call us to them, uplift us to self-sacrifice and heroic courage, that in all things both small and great we may be imitators of your dear Son, even Jesus Christ our Lord.

Christina Rosetti 1830–94

Keep our hearts, Lord, in that realm of the Spirit where the mind is without fear and the head is held high, where knowledge is wide, where words come from the depths of truth; where tireless striving wins towards perfection; where the clear stream of reason loses not its way but flows on in deeper thought and ever-widening action. Grant this, O Lord, for the honour of your Son Jesus Christ. AMEN

Thus said the Lord: Fear not: for I have redeemed you, I have called you by your name, you are mine. Fear not: for I am with you.

Isaiah 43

O God, our Father, you know how often we fail because we are afraid. We fear what men will do if we stand for the right; we fear what they will say. We fear that we shall not have strength to go on, even if we begin. Forgive us for our weakness. Help us to remember our Master Christ and all that he endured for us, so that we, like him, may never be afraid of men but only of sinning against your love. We ask it for his name's sake.

A. G. Pite

O Lord, in all the hazards of life, grant us courage which stands not in the strength of the arm, but in the stay of a good conscience. Be near to us when we are afraid; teach us when we should speak, and when we should be silent; when we must do, and when we must forbear; in all time of our temptation, danger and difficulty, let us not fall from you, who never fail them that trust your care, through Jesus Christ our Lord.

W. Charter Piggott

O God, give us courage – courage to make experiments and not be afraid of making mistakes; courage to get up when we are down; courage to work with all our might for the coming of your kingdom on earth, through Jesus Christ our Lord. AMEN

Encourage and strengthen us, O Father, for the days which lie ahead. Teach us to be humble, forgiving one another, even as Christ secured our forgiveness. Teach us to bear one another's burdens to fulfil his will. Teach us to learn from the devotion of those who have gone before how to spend and be spent in thy service. Day by day, may we grow in thy grace, and in the knowledge of each other: through Jesus Christ our Lord.   AMEN

vi *Confidence*

Almighty God, without whom nothing is strong, nothing is holy, may our speaking and hearing at this time be to the increase of faith, hope and love. May all that is untrue perish in the speaking, and all that is true be preserved for our use and your service; through Jesus Christ our Lord.   AMEN

Devotional Service

Grant that no word may fall from me against my will unfit for the present need.

Pericles BC 495 ?–429

Forgive me Lord, for having spoken so badly.
Forgive me for having spoken often to no purpose;
Forgive me for the days when I tarnished my lips with
hollow words,
false words,
cowardly words,
words through which you could not pass.
Uphold me when I must speak in a meeting, intervene in a
discussion, talk with a brother.
Grant above all, Lord, that my words may be like the sowing of seeds,
and that those who hear them may look to a fine harvest.

Michel Quoist 1918–

Noon: Calling

Dear God, it is so hard for us not to be anxious,
we worry about work and money,
about food and health,
about weather and crops,
about war and politics,
about loving and being loved.
Show us how perfect love casts out fear.

Monica Furlong

God, give me sympathy and common sense
and help me home with courage high.
God, give me calm and confidence
and please, a twinkle in my eye.

Margaret Bailey

NIGHT

It is not night if Thou be near.

John Keble

I
TESTING

i *Grey Days*

God of our life there are days when the burdens we carry chafe our shoulders and weigh us down: when the road seems dreary and endless, the skies grey and threatening: when our lives have no music in them, and our hearts are lonely, and our souls have lost their courage. Flood the path with light, we beseech you, tune our hearts to brave music; give us the sense of comradeship with heroes and saints of every age; and so quicken our spirits that we may be able to encourage the souls of all who journey with us on the road of life, to your honour and glory.   AMEN

Grant, Lord, that I may never run into those temptations which in my prayers I desire to avoid.   AMEN

Bishop Wilson

Grant us, O Lord our God, ever to find in thee a very present help in
   trouble.
When we are in the darkness of doubt or perplexity,
shed thy light upon our way.
When we are burdened with the affairs of our daily life,
lift us to the calm of thy presence.
When we are battling with temptation and the flesh is weak,
by the light of thy Spirit make us strong to overcome.
We ask these things through him in whom we are more than
   conquerors,
thy Son Jesus Christ our Lord.   AMEN

> The Lord watch between me and you
> when we are absent one from another.

Genesis 31:49

Short Prayers for the Long Day

Lord Jesus, we beseech Thee, by the loneliness of Thy suffering on the Cross, be nigh unto all them that are desolate and in pain or sorrow today; and let Thy presence transform their loneliness into comfort, consolation, and holy fellowship with Thee. Thou pitiful Saviour. AMEN

You cannot prevent the birds of sadness from flying over your head, but you can prevent them from building nests in your hair.

Chinese Proverb

Lord, your creation continues, yet, in nature
and by the hand of man.
Does this too cease when man is sixty-five?
Look on his loneliness,
his feeling of un-use.
Watching others off to earn their daily bread
and he still,
mourning his loss of opportunity
to worship through labour at the thing he knows best.
Find for him, Lord, a new dignity in quieter places.
Let him still give, not necessarily of his skill,
but of the fruit of all his years,
And be wanted,
    and needed,
        for a little while yet.
            Lord?

Roger Bush, *Prayers for Pagans*

ii *Trouble*

O God of Love, who art in all places and times, pour the balm of
thy comfort upon every lonely heart. Have pity upon those who
are bereft of human love, and on those to whom love has never come.
Be unto them a strong consolation, and in the end, give them fulness
of joy, for the sake of Jesus Christ, thy Son, our Lord.   AMEN

> O God the sea is so wide and my boat is so small:
> Be good to me.
>
> A Breton Fisherman

> What makes loneliness and anguish is not
> that I have no one to share my burden,
> but this,
> I have only my own burden to bear.
>
> Dag Hammarskjold 1905-61, *Markings*

Let us throw open the whole of our being to the influence of God's
forgiving love, asking him to deliver us
from dread of the unknown future,
from dread of illness or poverty,
from dread of loneliness,
from dread of death,
from dread of trials and sorrow for those we love,
from dread of what other people may think of us,
from dread of criticism, misunderstanding and ridicule,
from dread of taking responsibility lest we make mistakes.
Let us ask the abiding Spirit of Love to increase in us the fear
which is reverence, and to overcome in us the fear that is cowardice

O Loving Spirit of God, give us serene and quiet hearts. In days of stress and anxiety give us your tranquillity, and even amid disaster hold us in your divine peace. **AMEN**

O God of earth and altar,
bow down and hear our cry,
our earthly rulers falter,
our people drift and die;
the walls of gold entomb us,
the swords of scorn divide,
take not thy thunder from us
but take away our pride.

From all that terror teaches,
from lies of tongue and pen,
from all the easy speeches
that comfort cruel men,
from sale and profanation
of honour and the sword,
from sleep and from damnation
deliver us, Good Lord!

Gilbert Keith Chesterton
1874–1936

iii *Sickness*

Most wise, most Loving Father, who hast so enjoined that upon thee we should cast all our cares, move us to meet a brother's grief beside him. Guide him safely through the dark valley of his pain and sorrow, that he may fear no evil, nor ever feel forgotten or forsaken. Then let thy loving spirit lead him forth, his courage deepened, and his whole hope in thee; through him, who knew all griefs, and yet rejoiced in spirit, our greatest Elder Brother. **AMEN**

Toc H Prayer

Father, I find it hard to accept this illness.
I am impatient.
I find it hard to speak to anyone.
I find it hard to talk to you.
I am wrapped up in pity and worry for myself.
I worry over my health.
I worry about the things I would like to do, ought to do, but now I
    can't.
At a time like this I find it hard
to believe in you
to trust in you
to love you.
And yet I want to believe, to trust, to love.
I know you really care for me.
I cast all my care upon you.
I leave myself entirely in your kind hands.
Not my will but yours be done.
Lord Jesus I think of the pains you endured for me.
The great sadness of the garden, your scourging and crowning, your
    cross, your death.
You had to suffer to enter into your glory.
The sufferings of this time are not to be compared with the glory that
    is to come.
In the strength of your Spirit I join my sufferings to yours
for the redemption of the world.
Lord Jesus Christ, Son of God, have mercy on me a sinner.

A Catholic Prayer Book, 1970

Breathe down, O Lord, upon all those who are bearing pain, thy
spirit of healing, thy spirit of life, thy spirit of peace and hope, of
love and joy, thy spirit of courage and endurance. Cast out from
them the spirit of anxiety and fear, grant them perfect confidence
and trust in thee, that in thy light they may see light.

Diana Ponsonby

iv *Evil*

Father of Light! to thee I call;
my soul is dark within;
Thou who canst mark the sparrow's fall
avert the death of sin.
Thou, who canst guide the wandering star,
who calm'st the elemental war,
whose mantle is yon boundless sky,
my thoughts, my words, my crimes forgive,
And, since I soon must cease to live,
instruct me how to die.

Lord Byron 1788–1824, *The Adieu*

O thou who art love, and who seest all the suffering, injustices and
misery which reign in this world, have pity, we implore thee, on
the work of thy hands. Look mercifully upon the poor, the oppressed
and all who are heavy laden with error, labour and sorrow. Fill our
hearts with deep compassion for those who suffer, and hasten the
coming of thy Kingdom of justice and truth.

Eugene Bersier

Lord, for the erring thought
not into evil wrought;
Lord, for the wicked will,
betrayed and baffled still;
For the heart from itself kept
our thanksgiving accept!
For ignorant hopes that were
broken at our blind prayer;
For pain, death, sorrow sent,
unto our chastisement;
For all loss of seeming good,
Quicken our gratitude!

William Dean Howells 1837–1920

What was Hiroshima like, Jesus, when the bomb fell? What went through the minds of mothers, what happened to the lives of children, what stabbed at the hearts of men when they were caught up in the sea of flame?

What was Auschwitz like, Jesus, when the crematoriums belched the stinking smoke of the burned bodies of people? When families were separated, the weak perished, the strong faced inhuman tortures of the spirit and the body? What was the concentration camp like, Jesus?

Tell us, Lord, that we, the living, are capable of the same cruelty, the same horror, if we turn our backs on you, our brother, and our other brothers. Save us from ourselves; spare us the evils of our heart's good intentions, unbridled and mad. Turn us from our perversions of love, especially when these are perpetrated in your name. Speak to us about war, and about peace, and about the possibilities for both in our very human hearts.

Malcolm Boyd

v *Suffering*

Lord, in Thy pierced hands
I lay my heart;
Lord, at Thy pierced feet
I choose my part;
Lord, in Thy wounded side
Let me abide.

May Jesus Christ, the King of Glory, help us to make the right use of all the suffering that comes to us, and offer to him in incense of a patient and trustful heart; for his Name's sake. AMEN

John Tauler *c* 12th, adapted

God is in all men, but not all men are in God –
and that is why they suffer.

Pandit Nehru 1889–1964

Short Prayers for the Long Day

Thanks be to thee, Lord Jesus Christ,
for all the benefits thou has given me,
for all the pains and insults thou has borne for me.
O most merciful Redeemer, Friend, and Brother,
may I know thee more clearly,
may I love thee more dearly,
may I follow thee more nearly.   **AMEN**

St Richard of Chichester 1197–1253

From tomorrow on I shall be sad.
From tomorrow on.
Not today. Today I will be glad.
And every day, no matter how bitter it may be,
I shall say:
From tomorrow on I shall be sad,
not today.

From a child in a Nazi Death Camp

Hold on in the darkness though no gleam of light breaks through.
Keep on dreaming dreams although they never quite come true.
Keep on moving forward though you don't know what's ahead.
Keep on keeping on though it's a lonely road ahead.

Keep on looking up towards the goal you have in view.
Keep on at the task God has given you to do.
Keep on in the hope that there are better times in store.
Keep on praying for the thing that you are waiting for.

Blessings come to those who in the turmoil of events
Seek to see the goodness of the Will of Providence.
Hold to this and never doubt. Keep head and spirits high.
You'll discover that the storm was only passing by.

Night: Deepening

Seek Love in the pity of another's woe,
In the gentle relief of another's care.
In the darkness of night and the winter's snow.
In the naked and outcast – seek love there.

William Blake 1757–1827

2

DEEPENING

i *Weakness*

O Tree of Calvary,
send thy roots deep down
into my heart.
Gather together the soil of my heart,
the sands of my fickleness,
the stones of my stubbornness,
the mud of my desires,
bind them all together,
O Tree of Calvary,
interlace them with thy strong roots,
entwine them with the network
of thy love.

Chandran Devanesen

He prayed for strength that he might achieve;
He was made weak that he might obey.
He prayed for wealth that he might do greater things;
He was given infirmity that he might do better things.
He prayed for riches that he might be happy;
He was given poverty that he might be wise.
He prayed for power that he might have the praise of men;

He was given infirmity that he might feel the need of God.
He prayed for all things that he might enjoy life;
He was given life that he might enjoy all things.
He received nothing that he asked for – all that he hoped for;
His prayer was answered – he was most blessed.

ii *Forgiveness*

O Lord,
remember not only the men and women of goodwill,
but also those of ill will.
But do not only remember the suffering they have inflicted on us,
remember the fruits we bought thanks to this suffering,
our comradeship, our loyalty, our humility,
the courage, the generosity,
the greatness of heart which has grown out of all this.
And when they come to judgement
let all the fruits that we have borne
be their forgiveness.   AMEN   AMEN   AMEN

4/89

> Written on a piece of wrapping paper
> near the body of a dead child in Ravensbruck
> where 92,000 women and children died

Almighty . . .
Forgive
my doubt,
my anger,
my pride.
By thy mercy
abase me,
in thy strictness
raise me up.

Dag Hammarskjold 1905–61 *Markings*

Night: Deepening

O Master Christ! You have loved us with an everlasting love:
You have forgiven us, trained us, disciplined us:
You have broken us loose and laid your commandments upon us:
You have set us in the thick of things and deigned to use us:
You have shown yourself to us, fed us, guided us:
Be graciously pleased to accept and forgive our efforts
And keep us your free bond slaves forever.

> Hands who touched the leper,
> touch my wounded heart;
> Hands who healed the blindman,
> heal my aching soul;
> Hands who cured the lame,
> mend my disjointed life;
> Hands who embraced all life,
> enfold me in your peace.
> Lord,
> merely touch and heal
> cure and forgive.

Giles Harcourt 1936–

The heart that forgives an injury is like the perforated shell of a mussel, which loses its wound with a pearl.

J. P. Richter

Forgive us our sins, O Lord; the sins of our present and the sins of our past, the sins of our souls, and the sins of our bodies, the sins which we have done to please ourselves and the sins which we have done to please others. Forgive us our casual sins and our deliberate sins, and those which we have laboured so to hide that we have hidden them even from ourselves. Forgive us, O Lord, forgive us all our sins, for the sake of thy Son our Saviour, Jesus Christ.

Thomas Wilson

O Lord Jesus, because, being full of foolishness, we often sin and have to ask pardon, help us to forgive as we would be forgiven, neither mentioning old offences committed against us, nor dwelling upon them in thought, nor being influenced by them in heart, but loving each other freely as thou freely lovest us; for thy name's sake. AMEN
Christina Rossetti 1830–94

iii *Reflection*

Look towards the light and the shadow of your burden will be behind you.

When I was young, I never knew
one half the things that now I do –
I never realized that fame
may prove an empty, hollow game –
that wealth, despite all it can do,
but rarely brings contentment too –
that beauty, though its power be strong,
will not hide emptiness for long.
I did not guess that every deed
writes on the face lines all may read.
I did not know, when I was young,
a sense of humour is among
life's greatest gifts, nor did I see
that understanding, sympathy,
of true, tried friends will still hold sway
when shallow loves have passed away.
I did not dream pain can lead higher –
that love is stronger than desire.

By the faith that the flowers show when they bloom unbidden,
by the calm of the river's flow to a goal that is hidden,
by the trust of the tree that clings to its deep foundation,

by the courage of wild birds' wings on the long migration,
wonderful secret of peace that abideth in Nature's breast,
teach me how to confide, and live my life, and rest.

iv *Retreat*

I would like to get away,
Walk, run, to another land.
I know that joy exists; I have seen it on singing faces.
I know that light exists; I have seen it in radiant eyes.
But, Lord, I cannot get away
for I love my prison even while I hate it,
for my prison is myself,
and I love myself, Lord.
I both love and loathe myself.
Lord, I can no longer find the door myself,
I grope around blindly,
I bump against the walls of myself, my own confines.
I hurt myself,
I am in pain.

Lord, Lord, do you hear me?
Lord, show me my door,
take me by the hand.
Open the door,
show me the Way,
the Path leading to joy, to light.

Michel Quoist 1918–

O God, from whom all holy desires, all good counsels, and all just
works do proceed; Give unto thy servants that peace which the
world cannot give; that our hearts may be set to obey thy commandments, and also that by thee, we, being defended from the fear of our
enemies, may pass our time in rest and quietness; through the merits
of Jesus Christ our Saviour. AMEN

The Book of Common Prayer

Human wisdom says, Don't put off until tomorrow
what can be done the same day.
But I tell you that he who knows how to put off until tomorrow
is the most agreeable to God.
He who sleeps like a child
is also he who sleeps like my darling Hope.
And I tell you, Put off until tomorrow
those worries and those troubles which are gnawing at you today,
and might very well devour you today.
Put off until tomorrow those sobs that choke you
when you see today's unhappiness,
those sobs that rise up and strangle you.
Put off until tomorrow those tears which fill your eyes and your head
flooding you, rolling down your cheeks.
Because between now and tomorrow, maybe I, God,
will have passed by your way . . .
Blessed is he who puts off, that is to say,
Blessed is he who hopes. And who sleeps.

Charles Péguy 1873–1914

v Quietening

Teach me O Lord,
in the midst of noise,
the bustle of business,
that you are there, near,
close by, even within the creative noise
I sometimes cannot bear:
That I can find quietness
and peace within,
to regain my strength and offer it to you,
for your glory's sake.   AMEN

Roger Bush
Prayers for Pagans

Night: Deepening

The Lord is my pace-setter, I shall not rush,
He makes me stop and rest for quiet intervals,
he provides me with images of stillness, which restore my serenity.
He leads me in the way of efficiency; through calmness of mind.
And his guidance is peace.
Even though I have a great many things to accomplish each day
I will not fret, for his presence is here.
His timelessness, his all-importance will keep me in balance.
He prepares refreshment and renewal in the midst of activity.
By anointing my mind with his oils of tranquillity,
My cup of joyous energy overflows.
Surely harmony and effectiveness shall be the fruits of my hours
For I shall walk in the pace of my Lord, and dwell in his house for ever.

> Toki Miyashina, a Japanese Woman:
> *Psalm 23 for Busy People: Deliverance from
> the North-European disease*

Here in the quietness, Lord, we are part of each other.
Closer than lovers and loving close.
Thanks, Lord, for being part of me, not just now,
but in all the hurly-burly of life,
for being present in the children's smile,
the old man's whine, the mother's care.
For being where men are, Lord,
but most of all,
for once
being man.　AMEN

> Roger Bush, *Prayers for Pagans*

Teach us to care and not to care.
Teach us to sit still.

> T. S. Eliot 1888–1965

Go placidly amid the noise and haste, and remember what peace there may be in silence. As far as possible without surrender be on good terms with all persons. Speak your truth quietly and clearly; and listen to others, even the dull and ignorant; they too have their story.

Avoid loud and aggressive persons, they are vexatious to the spirit. If you compare yourself with others, you may become vain and bitter; for always there will be greater and lesser persons than yourself.

Enjoy your achievements as well as your plans. Keep interested in your own career, however humble; it is a real possession in the changing fortunes of time. Exercise caution in your business affairs; for the world is full of trickery. But let this not blind you to what virtue there is; many persons strive for high ideals; and everywhere life is full of heroism.

Be yourself. Especially do not feign affection. Neither be cynical about love; for in the face of all aridity and disenchantment it is perennial as the grass.

Take kindly the counsel of the years, gracefully surrendering the things of youth. Nurture strength of spirit to shield you in sudden misfortune. But do not distress yourself with imaginings. Many fears are born of fatigue and loneliness.

Beyond a wholesome discipline, be gentle with yourself. You are a child of the universe, no less than the trees and the stars; you have a right to be here. And whether or not it is clear to you, no doubt the universe is unfolding as it should.

Therefore be at peace with God, whatever you conceive him to be, and whatever your labours and aspirations, in the noisy confusion of life keep peace with yourself.

With all its sham, drudgery and broken dreams, it is still a beautiful world. Be careful, strive to be happy.

Old St Paul's, Baltimore, Maryland, 1692

1. A little more patience – to tolerate those with whom I must live and who are not at all congenial to me.
2. A little firmness – to continue this work which duty demands but which is repellant to me.
3. A little more humility – to remain at the post to which God has led me but which does not correspond with my dreams and plans.
4. A little more common sense – to take people as they are, not as I should like them to be.
5. A little more prudence – not to bother so much about other people's own business.
6. A little more strength – to endure that which so suddenly disturbs the soul.
7. A little more cheerfulness – so as not to show I have been hurt.
8. A little more unselfishness – in trying to understand the thoughts and feelings of others.
9. Above all, a little more prayer, to draw God to my heart and take counsel with him.

Nine Spiritual Remedies

vi *Meditating*

O Loving Spirit of our God who dwellest within us, warm and illumine every part of our being that the cold, dark shadow of fear, which shrinks from life's tasks and opportunities, may have no room for dwelling in the radiance of your light, which is love and peace and power. AMEN

O Lord, most glorious Lamb of God, most tender priest of man, who feedest thine own with the bread that cometh down from heaven, in whose hands is a cup, and the wine is red: We pray thee with this food and drink, so to satisfy our hunger that we hunger yet more, and our thirst that it never be quenched, but in thee, who livest and reignest, world without end. AMEN

O Christ, our only saviour, so dwell within us that we may go forth with the light of hope in our eyes, and the fire of inspiration on our lips, your word on our tongue, and your love in our hearts. AMEN

God, who blessest those that love thee and makest them holy that put their trust in thee, pour down thy grace on all who here today or in times past have by our side received thy sacred mysteries. Pardon the imperfections of our worship. Give us the best desire of our hearts, according to thy will and to our own needs, as thou alone knowest them. Grant that not one of us may fall short of thy Kingdom. May we so persevere in thy Grace that finally we may enter into thy Glory. Through Jesus Christ our saviour and friend.   AMEN

Strengthen for service, Lord, the hands that have taken holy things. May the ears that have heard your word never listen to discord. Keep from carelessness the tongues that expressed your praise; let the eyes which saw the signs of your love behold the fulness of your Kingdom; do not banish from your presence the feet that stood in your assembly; fill with new life the bodies fed by your body.

> From the Syrian Liturgy of Malabar, used in
> Experiment & Liturgy, Anglican Catholic Church of Canada

Jesus, we're here again. What are we doing here? I mean, how is communion with you possible? You're holy, and we're very human. Yet I remember that you also became human.

I wonder how we can honestly be nourished and cleansed by your body and blood. Yet I realize communion is an outward and visible sign of an inward and spiritual grace. I accept this mystery.

We are grateful for this intimacy with you, Jesus. We thank you for letting us share this corporate action as we offer to God all of creation including our lives. Give us faith to understand what it means to be thankful.

> Malcolm Boyd

Splintered rock and broken bread
when will you heal me?
Dried up stream and empty cup
when will you fill me?
Emptied desert and city street
how can you use me?

Weakened Lord and humble king
heal me, fill me, use me
now
for only then
will the rock become firm
the cup fill
the desert flower
and the city live.
And only then will
the rock become a mountain
and the mountain glory.
Then the length and breadth
and height and depth of
our souls will reach the transcended *now*
which is for ever
with him at the one point
where all points meet,
here.

Splintered rock and broken bread
when will you heal me?
Upon the mountain and here and . . . Now.

Giles Harcourt 1936–
'Symbols for Man: Rock, River,
Desert, City, Mountain'

vii *Wisdom*

Let us pray for a sense of balance and proportion in our daily life, and for the saving grace of humour.

'Methinks there is in God a well of laughter, very deep.'

God of all strength and harmony, teach us to find the deep springs of laughter in generosity and understanding. Give to us, we pray, the grace and courage of laughter that seeks to heal and not to hurt; that sees the unimportance of trifles instead of magnifying them; that gives us a sense of proportion by helping us to see not ourselves but yourself at the centre of all things. We ask this in the name of him who is the Lord of joy, Christ Jesus our Lord. **AMEN**

Lord you have entered and do ever enter into our common life, increase in us the grace to laugh generously with others and to be ready to laugh at ourselves. Save us from all false piety, from self-pity, from being dull and ponderous. Give to us your good gifts of gaiety, kindliness, and good humour. We ask it for your name's sake. **AMEN**

The Measure of a man
is not determined by his show of outward strength,
or the volume of his voice, or the thunder of his action.
It is to be seen, rather, in terms of the strength of his commitments,
the genuineness of his friendships, the sincerity of his purpose,
the quiet courage of his convictions,
his capacity to suffer,
and his willingness to continue 'growing up'.

Grady E. Poulard

A conscience that has been entrusted to God grows extraordinarily tender.

Brother Roger C.R., *So easy to love*

God has created me to do him some definite service. He has committed some work to me which he has not committed to another. I have my mission. I may never know it in this life, but I shall be told it in the next.

I am a link in a chain, a bond of connection between persons. He has not created me for naught. I shall do good. I shall do his work. I shall be an angel of peace, a preacher of truth in my own place while not intending it – if I do but keep his commandments.

Therefore, I will trust him. Whatever, wherever I am. I can never be thrown away. If I am in sickness, my sickness may serve him; in perplexity, my perplexity may serve him; if I am in sorrow, my sorrow may serve him. He does nothing in vain. He knows what he is about. He may take away my friends, he may throw me among strangers. He may make me feel desolate, make my spirits sink, hide my future from me – still he knows what he is about.

John Henry Newman 1801-90

A man of highest virtue
will not display it as his own;
His virtue then is real . . .
High virtue is at rest:
It knows no need to act.
Low virtue is a busyness
pretending to accomplishment.

from the *Tao Te Ching:* No. 38
translated by R. B. Blakney

It was Crane who once said that he had met many near-great men but few truly great – most of them lacked the white crown of humility. 'Your really great man,' he said, 'is always a little above praise, just a step beyond reward.'

The Wise Man's office
is to work by being still;
he teaches not by speech
but by accomplishment;
he does for everything,
neglecting none;
Life he gives to all,
possessing none;
And what he brings to pass
depends on no one else.
As he succeeds
he takes no credit
and just because he does not take it,
credit never leaves him.

... When you know
what eternally is so,
you have stature.
And stature means righteousness.
And righteousness is kingly.
And kingliness divine.
And divinity is the Way
which is final.

Then, though you die,
you shall not perish.

from the *Tao Te Ching:* No. 2, 16
translated by R. B. Blakney

The gentle way
will overcome.

from the *Tao Te Ching:* No. 36
translated by R. B. Blakney

3

REDEEMING

i *Silence*

Be still before the Lord, and wait patiently for him.

Psalm 37

My soul truly waits still upon God, for of him comes my salvation.

Psalm 62:1

In stillness and in staying quiet, there lies your strength.

Isaiah 30:15 NEB

In quietness and confidence shall be your strength.

Isaiah 30:15 AV

Lord, the noise of life is oppressing me,
the bother of life obstructing me,
the gossip of life overwhelming.
In the quietness of this evening hour, I ask you to
close my ears
so I may listen for silence,
close my eyes
so I may see your presence,
close my mouth
so that your words may speak to me clearly.
Calm my body, cleanse my heart,
and rest my soul,
that in waiting on you,
I may rest in you,
peacefully, quietly,
still.   Giles Harcourt 1936–

Give me thy grace, good Lord,
to set the world at naught;
To set my mind fast upon thee,
and not to hang upon the blast of men's mouths;
To be content to be solitary;
Not to long for worldly company;
Little and little utterly to cast off the world,
and rid my mind of all the business thereof;
Not to long to hear of any worldly things,
but that the hearing of worldly phantasies
may be to me displeasant;
Gladly to be thinking of God;
Piteously to call for his help;
To lean unto the comfort of God;
Busily to labour to love him;
To know mine own vility and wretchedness;
To humble and meeken myself
under the mighty hand of God;
To bewail my sins passed;
For the purging of them patiently to suffer adversity;
Gladly to bear my purgatory here;
To be joyful of tribulations;
To walk the narrow way that leadeth to life;
To bear the cross with Christ;
To have the last thing in remembrance;
To have ever afore mine eyes my death that is ever at hand.
To make death no stranger to me;
To foresee and consider the everlasting fire of hell;
To pray for pardon before the judge come;
To have continually in mind the passion that Christ suffered for me;
For his benefits uncessantly to give him thanks;
To buy the time again that I before have lost;
To abstain from vain confabulations.

These minds are more to be desired of every man than all the treasure of all the princes and kings, christian and heathen, were it gathered and laid together all upon one heap.

Sir Thomas More 1478–1535, *Book of Hours 1530*

Lord, show us deeply how important it is to be useless.

Bangkok prayer

Lord, temper with tranquillity,
my manifold activity.
That I may do my work for Thee,
with ever great simplicity.

ii *Time*

Lord, I have time
I have plenty of time.
All the time that you give me,
the years of my life,
the days of my years,
the hours of my days,
they are all mine.
Mine to fill, quietly, calmly,
but to fill completely, up to the brim,
to offer them to you, that of their insipid water
you may make a rich wine such as you made once in Cana of Galilee.
I am not asking you tonight, Lord, for time to do this and that, but
for your grace to do conscientiously, in the time that you give me,
what you want me to do.

Michel Quoist 1918–

Short Prayers for the Long Day

Take time to read,
take time to think:
it is the road to wisdom.
Take time to laugh,
take time to love,
it is the road to being alive.
Take time to give,
take time to pray:
it is the way to God.

Christ was never in a hurry. And if God has given us anything to do for him, he will give time enough to finish it with a repose like Christ's.

Henry Drummond 1786–1860

iii *Prayer*

Hallowed be Thy name,
not mine,
thy kingdom come,
not mine,
Give us peace with Thee,
peace with men,
peace with ourselves,
And free us from all fear.

Dag Hammarskjold 1905–61
Markings

Four things which are not in thy treasury,
I lay before thee, Lord, with this petition:
My nothingness, my wants,
my sins, and my contrition.

Robert Southey 1774–1843

O Thou, whom to forget is to stumble and fall, whom to remember
is to rise again. Set Thy seal upon this work, that many more may
know their need of Thee, Thy need of them; Christ Jesus, Lord.

AMEN

Lift up our hearts, we beseech thee, O Christ, above the false show
of things, above fear, above laziness, above selfishness and covetousness, above custom and fashion, up to the everlasting truth and order
that thou art; so that we may live joyfully and freely, in faithful trust
that thou art our Saviour, our example and our friend, in this world
and in the world to come.

Charles Kingsley 1819–75

Religion is in the heart
Not in the knees.

Douglas Jerrold

From the point of Light within the mind of God,
let light stretch forth into the minds of men,
let light descend on earth.
From the point of love within the heart of God,
let love stream forth into the hearts of men:
may Christ return to earth.
From the centre where the will of God is known,
let purpose guide the little wills of men:
the purpose which the Master knows and serves.
From the centre which we call the race of men,
let the plan of love and light work out,
and may it seal the door where evil dwells.
Let light and love and power restore the plan on earth.

Hope is one of your best gifts to us.
Teach us to give it to others.

Short Prayers for the Long Day

I ask and wish not to appear
more beauteous, rich or gay.
Lord, make me wiser every year,
and better every day.

Charles Lamb 1775–1834

Action should be something added to the life of prayer,
not something taken away from it.

St Thomas Aquinas 1225–74

O God, give me the sincerity to accept the things I cannot change,
the courage to change the things I can,
and the wisdom to know the difference.

Rheinhold Niebuhr 1892–1971

Lord of sincerity and truth, may the cleansing wind of your reality
strip from us all foolish pretences, all insincerity of mind and heart.
Make us fully alive to things as they really are, whether they be
pleasant or unpleasant, and give us courage never to shrink from
experiencing them to the full. We ask it for your name's sake.

AMEN

O God who art the light of the minds that know thee, the life of the
souls that love thee, and the strength of the hearts that serve thee;
help us to know thee that we may truly love thee; so to love thee
that we may fully serve thee, whom to serve is perfect freedom;
through Jesus Christ our Lord.   AMEN

Gelasian Sacramentary

To know what you prefer, instead of saying AMEN to what the
world tells you you ought to prefer, is to have kept your soul alive.

R. L. Stevenson 1850–94

Night: Redeeming

I thank you, Lord
for knowing me better than
I know myself
and for letting me know myself
better than others know me.
Make me, I ask you then,
better than they suppose.
And forgive me for what
they do not know.

Abu Bakr c 572–634

Prayer to a heart of lowly love
opens the gate of heaven above.
Ah, prayer is God's high dwelling place.
From earth to heaven we build a stair –
the name by which we call it, prayer.
Prayer is the gracious Father's knee;
on it the child climbs lovingly.
Love's rain, the Spirit's holy ray
and tears of joy are theirs who pray.
To walk with God, to feel His kiss,
yes, prayer, His servant owns, is this.

N. V. Tilak

Lord, I am stiff and rigid in my prayers. I need to loosen up. To talk
to you as a human being. To discuss my problems and my fears with
you. To behave as a disciple and not as a distant admirer, setting you
on a pedestal where I feel sure you have no desire to be. I would like
very much to enjoy my prayers. To feel as relaxed as I do when taking
a walk in the country. I would like to enjoy my communion with
you as much as I enjoy a piece of good music or a good ballet. I must
make my mind work at my prayer so that I can bring everything
into it. I know you are interested. It is I who am dull and stiff and
'mannered'. Humanize me, Lord.

Norman Goodacre

None is so near God as he who shows kindness.

Seneca c AD 65

Eternal Light, shine into our hearts;
Eternal Goodness, deliver us from evil;
Eternal Power, be our support;
Eternal Wisdom, scatter the darkness of our ignorance;
Eternal Pity, have mercy upon us;
that with all our hearts and mind and soul and strength we may seek thy face and be brought by thine infinite mercy to thy holy presence; through Jesus Christ our Lord.

Alcuin c 735–804

iv *Deliverance*

Peace does not mean the end of all our striving.
Joy does not mean the drying of our tears.
Give me, for light, the sunshine of Thy sorrow.
Give me, for shelter, the shadow of Thy cross;
Give me to share the glory of Thy morrow,
gone from my heart the bitterness of loss.

G. A. Studdart Kennedy 1883–1929

Be this the central faith and fact of life: that there is a light beyond our darkness, and a purpose which makes music of our confusion – and we, you and I have some part in both. Hold fast to that and fear nothing.

Gerald Bullett

Lord Jesus Christ, you have power of life and death, of health and sickness; give power, wisdom, and gentleness to all physicians and surgeons, nurses and watchers by the sick, that always bearing about your presence with them, they may not only heal but bless, and shine as lamps of hope in the darkest hours of distress and fear. Through Jesus Christ our Lord. AMEN

Grant, O Lord, that because we meet together here this day, life may grow sweeter for some who are confused by it, happier for some who are tasting the bitterness of it, safer for some who are feeling the peril of it, more friendly for some who are feeling the loneliness of it, serener for some who are throbbing with the fever of it, holier for some for whom life has lost all dignity, beauty and meaning; through Jesus Christ our Lord.   AMEN

> If you pour yourself out for the hungry
> and satisfy the desire of the afflicted
> then shall your light rise in the darkness
> and your gloom be as the noonday
> and the Lord will guide you continually
> and you shall be like a watered garden
> like a spring of water
> whose waters fail not.
>
> Isaiah 58: 9–11

v *Graces*

May God relieve the wants of others and give us thankful hearts; for Christ's sake.

John Dallas

Heavenly Father, make us thankful to thee and mindful of others as we receive these blessings, in Jesus' name.

Book of Common Worship

Lord, make us thankful for these and all your other mercies, through Jesus Christ our Lord.

We thank you, O Lord, for this food and for all your love, through Jesus Christ our Lord.

Short Prayers for the Long Day

Lord, for these and for all your gifts, we give you thanks.

In thanks to God for all his benefits:
Let us have a moment's silence for
the hungry of the world.

What God gives, and what we take,
'tis a gift for Christ his sake;
Be the meal of beans and peas,
God be thanked for those, and these.
Have we flesh, or have we fish,
all are fragments from his dish.
He his Church save, and the king,
and our peace here, like a spring,
make it ever flourishing.

Robert Herrick 1591-1674

God is great and God is good
and we thank him for our food.
By his hand we all are fed.
Give us, Lord, our daily bread.
AMEN

Thou that has given so much to me,
Give one thing more – a grateful heart;
Not thankful when it pleases me,
As if thy blessings had spare days;
But such a heart, whose very pulse may be
Thy praise.

George Herbert 1593-1633

Listen, and I will tell you who are the Happy People whom God has blessed. Happy are the poor, for nothing stands between them and the Kingdom. Happy are the sorrowful, for their souls are made strong through suffering. Happy are the humble, for they receive the whole world as a gift. Happy are they who long for holiness as a man longs for food, for they shall enjoy God's plenty. Happy are the merciful, for they are mercifully judged. Happy are they who establish peace for they share God's very nature. Happy are the single-hearted, for they see God.

Dorothy L. Sayers from *The Man Born to be King*

Hail King! Hail King!
Blessed is he; Blessed is he;
Bless this house and all that it contains,
From rafter and stone and beam,
Deliver to God from pole to cover,
Be the healing of men therein.
Hail King! Hail King!
Blessed is he; Blessed is he;
Without beginning, without ending,
Every generation for aye.
Ho! Hi! Let there be joy.

A House Blessing
from the Celtic

May Almighty God dispose your days in his peace,
and grant you the gift of his blessing.
May he set you free from all anxiety,
and settle your mind(s) in tranquillity and peace
that adorned with the jewels of faith, hope and charity
you may pass without harm through this present life,
and come in safety to your eternal home.   AMEN

Short Prayers for the Long Day

Blessed be the roof of stars
and all the journeys further.
Blessed be the blindfold journey up the stairs
in the arms of my father.

Blessed be the poor man's food
bought with begged farthings.
Blessed be the dancing heels
of my May darling.

Blessed be the cup of flour
daily turned to bread.
Blessed be the holy living:
blessed be the humble dead.

Blessed be the vine
climbing the warm stone.
Blessed be the fearful going out:
blessed be the coming home.

Blessed be the humble hands
that take bread.
Blessed be the singing eyes
that taste wine.

Blessed be the poor hands
that feel the body in the bread.
Blessed be the pure eyes
that see tears in the wine.

Holy was the bread: body divine.
Holy were the tears, shed in the wine.
Holy is the life blood, soon to be mine.

David Scott

May the Lord Jesus Christ who is the splendour of the eternal light, drive from your hearts all darkness, and may the blessing of God Almighty, the Father, the Son, and the Holy Spirit, rest upon you and upon all your work done in his name, now and always. AMEN

> May the grace of Christ uphold you,
> and the Father's love enfold you,
> may the Holy Spirit guide you,
> and all the joy and peace betide you,
> now and to eternity.   AMEN

Now unto him that is able to keep us from falling, and to present us faultless before the presence of his glory, with exceeding joy, to the only wise God, our Saviour, be glory and majesty, dominion and power, both now and forever.   AMEN

Jude 24–5

Now unto him that hath loved us and loosed us from our sins in his own blood, and hath made us to be kings and priests with God the Father, to him be the glory and dominion for ever and ever. AMEN

Revelation 1: 5b–6

> Unto God's gracious mercy and protection we commit you.
> The Lord bless you and keep you:
> The Lord make his face to shine upon you,
> and be gracious unto you:
> The Lord lift up the light of his countenance upon you
> and give you peace
> both now and for evermore.

Based on Numbers 6:24–26

And now unto Him who is able to keep us from falling and lift us from the dark valley of despair to the bright mountain of hope, from the midnight of desperation to the daybreak of joy; to Him be power and authority, for ever and ever.

Martin Luther King 1929–68

Lord, as men sleep, purge out of every heart the lurking grudge.
Cause injuries to be forgot and benefits to be remembered. Frustrate
the evil will of man; and in all of good, further their endeavours.
Make it heaven about them, Lord, by the only way to heaven,
forgetfulness of self. Let peace abound in our great company.
Recreate in and through thy Holy Church the spirit of service, the
soul of peace, the sense of joy. May we be brave in peril, constant in
tribulation; and in all changes of fortune and down to the gates of
death, loyal and loving one to another, through Jesus Christ our
Lord. AMEN

Toc H Prayer

> Before the ending of the day,
> Creator of the world we pray,
> That with Thy wonted favour thou
> wouldst be our guard and keeper now.
>
> From all ill dreams defend our eyes,
> from nightly fears and fantasies;
> tread under foot our ghostly foe,
> that no pollution we may know.
>
> O Father, that we ask be done,
> through Jesus Christ, thine only Son;
> Who with the Holy Ghost and thee,
> doth live and reign eternally.   AMEN

From *Compline*

Lord, support us all the day long in this troublous life, until the
shades lengthen, the evening comes, the busy world is hushed, the
fever of life is over, and our work is done. Then, Lord, in your
mercy grant us safe lodging, a holy rest, and peace, at the last, through
Jesus Christ our Lord. AMEN

John Henry Newman 1801–90

O God, who by making night succeed the day hast bestowed on human weakness the gift of rest and sleep: Grant us so to enjoy these timely blessings; that we fail not to acknowledge Thee from Whom they come; Who art blessed and dost live and govern all things world without end. AMEN

O Lord, we thank you, at the close of another day for the example of your cross which, as a focus of reconciliation, shows us how to live our lives in obedience to your will, by disowning fear and discouragement, cynicism and despair, and by discarding tiredness, tension, intolerance and self-concern.

We thank you for the divine gift of humour which enables us to see, in part, ourselves through your eyes; we thank you also for the joy we can give to each other if only we try, for the numerous interests that can be mutually shared, and the hopes we can help to fulfil by giving up ourselves to your service and by striving to walk cheerfully and uprightly with you each day of our lives. Conscious of our shortcomings we make this offering in the name of our Friend, your only Son Jesus Christ. AMEN

Giles Harcourt 1936–

God keep my heart attuned to laughter when youth is done;
When all the days are grey days, coming after the warmth, the sun.
Ah! Keep me then from bitterness, from grieving, when life seems cold;
God keep me always loving and believing as I grow old. AMEN

This evening, Lord, I am afraid.
I am afraid, for your Gospel is terrible.
It is easy to hear it preached,
it is relatively easy not to be shocked by it,
but it is very difficult to live it.

Michel Quoist 1918–

Now that the day doth end,
my spirit I commend,
to thee, my Lord, my Friend.
Into thy hands, yea, thine,
those glorious hands benign
my spirit I resign.

Our Father, in these hours of daylight we remember those who must wake that we may sleep: bless those who watch over us at night, the guardians of the peace, the watchers who save us from the terror of fire, and all the many who carry on through the hours of the night, the restless commerce of men on land and sea. We thank thee for their faithfulness and sense of duty; we pray thee for thy pardon if our covetousness or luxury make their nightly toil necessary: grant that we may realize how dependent the safety of our loved ones and the comforts of life are on these our brothers, that so we may think of them with love and gratitude and help to make their burden lighter. Through Jesus Christ our Lord.   AMEN

Preserve us O Lord while waking
and guard us while sleeping.
That awake we may watch with Christ
and asleep we may rest in peace.

From *Compline*

Into thy hands, O Lord, I commend my spirit, this night and forevermore.   AMEN

viii *Christmas*

O Father, who hast declared thy love to men by the birth of the holy child at Bethlehem; help us to welcome him with gladness and to make room for him in our common days; so that we may live at peace with one another and in goodwill with all thy family; through the same thy Son, Jesus Christ our Lord.

A Devotional Diary

Night: Redeeming

C ourage to act
H ope to light the way
R emembrance of the lonely among us
I deals for those who follow
S ympathy for need and trouble
T houghtfulness
M erriment
A ppreciation of this past year's blessings
S ecurity in God.

David Cory

Give us, O God, the vision which can see Thy love in the world in spite of human failure.

Give us the faith, the trust, the goodness in spite of our ignorance and weakness.

Give us the knowledge that we may continue to pray with understanding hearts, and show us what each one of us can do to set forth the coming of the day of universal peace.   AMEN

Frank Borman, 'An Astronaut's Christmas Prayer'
(in orbit round the moon)

Let us pray that strength and courage abundant be given to all who work for a world of reason and understanding;

That the good that lies in every man's heart may day by day be magnified;

That men will come to see more clearly not that which divides them, but that which unites them;

That each hour may bring us closer to a final victory, not of nation over nation, but of man over his own evils and weaknesses;

That the true spirit of this Christmas season – its joy, its beauty, its hope, and above all its abiding faith – may live among us;

That the blessings of peace be ours – the peace to build and grow, to live in harmony and sympathy with others, and to plan for the future with confidence.

New York Life Insurance Company

Short Prayers for the Long Day

May the humility of the shepherds
the perseverance of the wise men
the joy of the angels and
the peace of the Christ Child
be God's gift to you this Christmastide and always.

Mervyn Stockwood

Love came down at Christmas,
love all lovely, love divine;
Love was born at Christmas,
stars and angels gave the sign.

Love shall be our token,
love be yours and love be mine,
love to God and all men,
love for plea and gift and sign.

Christina Rossetti 1830–94

Be thou a bright flame before me,
Be thou a guiding star above me,
Be thou a smooth path below me,
Be thou a kindly shepherd behind me,
Today – tonight – and forever.

St Columba of Iona c 521–97

4

PERFECTING

i *Age*

They shall grow not old, as we that are left grow old:
Age shall not weary them, nor the years condemn.
At the going down of the sun and in the morning
We will remember them.

Laurence Binyon 1869–1943

Night: Perfecting

Some there are who have left a name behind them to be com-
  memorated in story.
There are others who are unremembered;
They are dead, and it is as though they had never existed,
as though they had never been born
or left children to succeed them.
Not so our forefathers; they were men of loyalty,
whose good deeds have never been forgotten . . .
Their bodies are buried in peace,
But their name lives for ever.
Nations will recount their wisdom,
And God's people will sing their praises.

Ecclesiasticus 44 (NEB)

God guard me from those thoughts men think
In the mind alone:
He that sings a lasting song
Thinks in a marrow-bone;

From all that makes a wise old man
That can be praised of all;
Oh, what am I that I should not seem
For the song's sake a fool?

I pray – for fashion's word is out
And prayer comes round again –
That I may seem, though I die old,
A foolish, passionate man.

W. B. Yeats 1865–1939

Jesus, who never grew old, it is not easy for any of us to face old age.
It is fine to be young, attractive, strong. Old age reminds us of weakness and dependence upon others. But to be your disciple means
accepting weakness and inter-dependence. Because of you we can
rejoice in weakness in ourselves, and be tender to it in others.

Monica Furlong

ii *Death*

Angrily spake the gardener,
'Who plucked this flower
one of the rarest in all my garden?'
Gently answered the Master,
'So dearly did I love it I chose it for my own.'

> Tread lightly, she is near
> under the snow,
> speak gently, she can hear
> the daisies grow.
>
> All her bright golden hair
> tarnished with rust.
> She that was young and fair
> fallen to dust.
>
> Lily-like, white as snow,
> she hardly knew
> she was a woman, so
> sweetly she grew.

Oscar Wilde 1856–1900

O God, thou will not leave us in the dust;
thou madest man, he knows not why.
He thinks he was not made to die
and thou hast made him; thou art just.

When the last sea is sailed, when the last shallow's charted,
when the last field is reaped, and the last harvest stored,
when the last fire is out and the last guest departed,
grant the last prayer that I shall pray, Be Good to me, O Lord!

John Masefield 1878–1967

Night: Perfecting

Man with his burning soul,
has but an hour to breathe.
To build a ship of truth,
in which his soul may sail –
sail on the sea of death;
for death takes toll
of beauty, courage, youth.
Of all but truth.

John Masefield 1878–1967

So be my passing!
My task accomplished and the long day done,
my wages taken, and in my heart
some late lark singing,
let me be gathered to the quiet west,
the sundown splendid and severe,
Death.

W. E. Henley 1849–1903

Death stands above me, whispering low
I know not what into my ear:
Of this strange language all I know
is, there is not a word of fear.

Walter Savage Landor 1775–1864

I shall remember while the light lives yet
And in the nightime I shall not forget.

A. C. Swinburne 1837–1909

He had the ploughman's strength in the grasp of his hand. He could
see a crow three miles away. He could hear the green oats growing,
and the southwest wind making rain. He could make a gate and dig a
ditch and plough as straight as a stone can fall. And he is dead.

E. Rhys

iii *Peace*

Peace is so hard to build
so easy to destroy.
Peace of mind
Peace of heart
Peace of home
Peace of land.
We thank you Lord this day
for all those who have given their lives in war
that we might live in peace,
and, in gratitude, become in turn living instruments of peace:
Peace in mind
Peace in heart
Peace in home
Peace in land.

Giles Harcourt 1936–

Deep peace of the Running Wave to you.
Deep peace of the Flowing Air to you.
Deep peace of the Quiet Earth to you.
Deep peace of the Shining Stars to you.
Deep peace of the Son of Peace to you.

11/89   Celtic Benediction

Peace I leave with you; my peace I give unto you.
Not as the world giveth, give I unto you.
Let not your heart be troubled, neither let it be afraid.

John 14:27

iv *Perspective*

The whole Creation is a perpetual ascension, from brute to man, from man to God. To divest ourselves more and more of matter, to be clothed more and more with Spirit, such is the law.

Victor Hugo 1802–85

Man dies daily when he sleeps, and yet he is not dead; and that death which comes at the end of every lifetime is merely a longer sleep than that which comes at the end of every day.

Tibetan Book of the Great Liberation

> Death be not proud, though some have called thee
> mighty and dreadful, for thou are not so;
> For those whom thou think'st thou dost overthrow
> die not, poor Death, nor yet canst thou kill me . . .
> One short sleep past, we wake eternally,
> and death shall be no more. Death, thou shalt die.

John Donne 1572–1631

The fear of death is indeed the pretence of wisdom, and not really wisdom, being a pretence of knowing the unknown; and no one knows whether death, which men in their fear apprehend to be the greatest evil, may not be the greatest good.

Socrates 469–399 BC

> If the Great Father Creator is as great as death,
> surely as creator of the universe, of darkness and light,
> he must be at least equal to his creation;
> and in so being,
> as an artist is greater than his canvas,
> so is he greater than death.

Giles Harcourt 1936–

The souls of the just are in the hand of God, and no torment shall touch them. In the eyes of the foolish they appear to be dead; their departure was reckoned as defeat, and their going from us as disaster. But they are at peace, for though in the sight of men they may be punished, they have a sure hope of immortality.

> Wisdom of Solomon 3: 1 NEB (adapted)

> Then shall I know:
> not till the loom is silent
> and the shuttles cease to fly
> shall God unroll the canvas
> and explain the reason why
> the dark threads are as needful
> in the weaver's skilful hand
> as the threads of gold and silver
> in the pattern he has planned.

So when this corruptible shall have put on incorruption, and this mortal shall have put on immortality, then shall be brought to pass the saying that is written, Death is swallowed up in victory. O Death, where is thy sting? O Grave, where is thy victory?

> I Corinthians 15:54-5

The man of Faith may face death as Colombus faced his first voyage from the shores of Spain. What lies beyond the seas he cannot tell: all his special expectations may be mistaken, but his insight into the clear meaning of present facts may persuade him beyond doubt that the sea has another shore.

> H. E. Fosdick 1878–1969

> They who bewail the certainty of death
> may be comforted by the promise of immortality to come.
> For to thy faithful people, O Lord, life is changed
> but not taken away.

> The Missal

v *Resurrection*

So the Master of the Garden took Bamboo and cut him down and hacked off his branches and stripped off his leaves and cleaved him in twain and cut out his heart. And lifting him gently, carried him to where there was a spring of fresh, sparkling water in the midst of the dry fields. Then putting one end of broken Bamboo in the spring and the other end into the water channel in his field, the Master laid down gently his beloved Bamboo. And the spring sang welcome and the clear sparkling waters raced joyously down the channel of Bamboo's torn body into the waiting fields. The rice was planted, and the days went by, and the shoots grew and the harvest came.

In that day was Bamboo, once so glorious in stately beauty, yet more glorious in his brokenness and humility. For in his beauty was life abundant, but in his brokenness he became a channel of abundant life to his Master's world.

Eric Hague

That man is a success who has lived well, laughed often, and loved much; who has gained the respect of intelligent men and the love of children; who has filled his niche and accomplished his task; who leaves the world better than he found it, whether by an improved poppy, a perfect poem or a rescued soul, who never lacked appreciation of Earth's beauty, or failed to express it; who looked for the best in others and gave the best he had; his memory is a benediction.

R. L. Stevenson 1850–94

I said to the man who stood at the Gate of the Year, 'Give me a light that I may tread safely into the unknown.' And he replied, 'Go out into the darkness and put your hand into the hand of God. That shall be to you better than light and safer than a known way.' May that almighty hand guide and uphold us all.

Minnie Haskins 1875–1957

Go forth upon thy journey from this world, O Christian soul,
in the peace of him in whom thou hast believed,
in the name of God the Father, who created thee,
in the name of Jesus Christ, who suffered for thee,
in the name of the Holy Spirit, who strengthened thee.
May angels and archangels, and all the armies of the heavenly host,
  come to meet thee,
may all the saints of God welcome thee,
may thy portion this day be in gladness and peace, thy dwelling in
  Paradise.
Go forth upon thy journey, O Christian Soul.

> Prayer for the dying, from the Roman Ritual

Christ is the morning star who
when the darkness of this world is past
brings to his saints
the promise of the light of life
and opens everlasting day.

> The Venerable Bede 673–735